Widgit Rebus Symbol Collection

Tina Detheridge, Helen Whittle, and Cate Detheridge

Widgit Software Ltd
124 Cambridge Science Park
Milton Road
Cambridge
CB7 0ZS, UK

**Widgit Software Ltd
124 Cambridge Science Park
Milton Road
Cambridge
CB4 0ZS, UK**

First published in Great Britain by Widgit Software Ltd. 2002

Copyright Widgit Software Ltd. 2002

ISBN 0-9539346-1-6

Typeset by Widgit Software Ltd,
Design by Cate Detheridge
Printed in Great Britain by the Panda Group

CONTENTS

6 Animals

7 Environment and Nature

8 Places

9 Countries

10 Sports

11 Recreation

12 Actions

13 Direction and Position

14 Time and Dates

15 Size

16 Shape

17 Colour and Appearance

18 Materials and their properties

19 Sound and Temperature

20 Food and Drink

21 Cooking and Eating

22 Buildings

23 Home, Interiors and Domestic Activities

24 Work and Equipment

25 Packaging

26 Shops, Shopping and Organisations

27 Money

28 Transport

29 Knowledge Communication

Acknowledgements to contributors to the new Widgit Rebus Symbol Collection

The project was co-ordinated by Helen Whittle, Speech and Language Therapist.
Drawings were done by Cate Detheridge

The consultative group
This group worked consistently throughout the 10 months of the development phase of the project. We are very grateful for the quality, consistency and speed of their responses throughout the project. Without them the work would not have reached such a high quality.

Frances Bodger and Julia Torode, Harrow Access & Development Team, Wealdstone
Sarah Clements, Freemantle School, Chertsey
Sharon Cowan, The Avenue School, Reading
Penny Dembo, South West PCT, Sheffield
Helen Dixon, George Hastwell School
Linda Edwards, NCYPE, Lingfield
Rowena Fellingham, Harrogate District Hospital, Harrogate
Anne Hancox, Specialist Speech & Language Therapy Team - ALD, Malvern Link
David Harley, Independent Consultant, Coventry
Gillian Hazell, ACE Centre, Oxford
Imogen Howarth and Elaine Orpe, SkillBase, Chelmsford
Jane Kinson, People in Partnership, Birmingham
Janet Larcher, Independent Consultant, Weybridge
Sue Lord, St Charles Hospital, London
Maureen Lymer, Ravensbourne NHS Trust, Farnborough
Sue Lyons and Jill Eddlestone, Leicester Frith Hospital, Leicester
Judy Melland, Independent Consultant, Bedford
Kay Mienertzhagen, Independent Consultant, Gillingham
Sally Millar, CALL Centre, Edinburgh
Judy Robertson, Independent Expressions, Knebworth
Nic Rowland-Crosby, Health Action Zone, Plymouth
Jackie Stubbs, Sarah Sherratt, Sarah Chandler, Claire Barge, New Possibilities NHS Trust, Colchester
Dominic Trounce, Learning Disability Service, Plymouth
Kate Ullman, Independent Consultant, Birmingham

The review group
In addition to the development group, a small number of additional people were invited to review the entire set of revisions. We are very grateful for their detailed and careful work.

Ann Aspinall, Home Farm Trust, Abingdon
Darren Banks, Community Resource Team, Hythe
Emma Jones, Addington Clinic, Bournemouth
Lindsey Lambert, Beverley Thorne & Naomi Mason, Communication Team, Kidderminster
Gill Lloyd, Independent Consultant, Leatherhead
Karen Newman, The Runnymede Centre, Addlestone
Sharon McKelvey, Strathmore School, Richmond
Dave Mitchell, Worcestershire County Council, Worcs
Sue Norton, Independent Consultant, Brighton
Kay Rickwood, Portesbery School, Camberley
Dave Wood, Independent Consultant, Rothwell

Judy van Oosterom
We are also pleased that Judy van Oosterom finds that the structural and design changes of the revised Widgit Rebus set clearly continues the work that she and Kathleen started so many years ago.

Acknowledgements to contributors to the original Rebus Symbol Collection.

The original Rebus Symbol Collection was developed by Judy van Oosterom and Kathleen Devereux, from the US Rebuses developed in Nashville, Tennessee.

The initial Rebus Glossary was developed in the UK by Judy van Oosterom and Kathleen Devereux. This set, comprising around 800 symbols was published in 1985 by LDA. During the period 1994 to 1998, Widgit worked closely with Judy van Oosterom to develop the symbols to reach a list of some 4000 items.

We are grateful to the following contributors to this collection:

Chailey Heritage School, in particular to Valerie Moffatt and Liz Meek.
> The Chailey heritage Symbol Collection, which used Rebus symbols, was developed in collaboration between Widgit and Chailey Heritage School to meet the needs of children and young adults with complex communication needs.

The Ken Jones Memorial project.
> Ken Jones worked for many years in teacher education at the University of the West of England (formerly Bristol University). Throughout his career he maintained a strong interest in the use of symbols to enhance reading. As a memorial to Ken, a project was set up to develop additional symbols for the Rebus Symbol Collection in the area of personal development.

Erica Brown
> Eric has long been involved in religious spiritual and moral education of children with special educational needs. Erica worked with members of six different faith groups to provide a core of symbols to promote inter-faith understanding.

Signalong
> Signalong have developed comprehensive signing vocabularies for people with learning difficulties. To compliment these signs Signalong and Widgit collaborated to develop additional symbols so that there are symbol equivalents for all of the signs in their basic vocabularies. In particular we are grateful to Kay Meinertzhagen and Jill Kennard for contribution to the designs.

Sue Norton
> Sue Norton is a teacher of science in a special school release. She developed the initial science symbols which were included in the Rebus Symbol Collection. We are very grateful to Sue for her continued interest in the symbol development and in new approaches to symbol use to support children with learning difficulties.

And also to David Banes, Wendy Newton, Clare Martin, Andy Carmichael and Judy Sebba for their advice and critical reviews of the earlier symbols.

Tina Detheridge,
Project Manager

Chapter 1: The Rebus Symbol Development Project

The new Widgit Rebus Symbols have been developed in collaboration with professionals, to meet the wide and changing needs of symbol users worldwide. This chapter describes the project and then goes on to discuss the implications for using them.

1.1 A brief history of Rebus Symbols and how they have developed

Symbols have been used to support the face-to-face communication of those with little or no speech since the early 1970's. More recently symbols have been used to support the development of literacy skills and the use of text by those whose ability with text is limited.

Rebus Symbols were first devised as part of the Peabody Rebus Reading Program in the USA in the 1960's. They were further developed in a UK school by Judy Van Oosterom and Kathleen Devereux to make them more applicable as a support for language development with pupils who had moderate or severe learning disabilities. This set was first published in booklet form by LDA in the UK.

With the advent of symbol software the development of the Rebus Symbols was, with Judy's support, gradually taken over by Widgit Software. There were also many contributions from other practitioners and organisations. Until the advent of the software the number of symbols was about 600. New libraries of symbols were brought out on a regular basis and added to as a result of requests from users of the symbols and from professionals supporting symbol users. At the start of the Rebus Symbol Development Project, in October 2000 there were 5000 symbols. The growth of the symbol set has, therefore, been extensive - but it has not always been consistent. The style of the symbol drawing has also changed over the years. These factors led Widgit Software to set up the Rebus Symbol Development Project to review the whole symbol set with a view to consistency. The new Symbol set will be known as the Widgit Rebus Symbol Set, to ensure that its identity is clear, especially as the extent of the use is growing internationally. We are grateful to Judy van Oosterom for her continued support for these developments from her original work as well as to the many professionals and users who have contributed over the years. A full list of acknowledgements to both the original Rebus Symbols Collection and this new Widgit Rebus set is given at the beginning of this book.

1.2 The need for consistency of symbols and their extension for literacy use

Rebus symbols have been used more recently as a support for literacy development. This has meant that there has been a need for an increased vocabulary. As a result there has been a demand that the symbols are constructed consistently so that when a number of symbols are printed out together they look good on the page and make coherent sense. The original system had developed in an ad hoc manner which did not always meet these criteria. The original schema was set out in "Literacy Through Symbols". However as the demand for an increased vocabulary grew these guidelines were not always adhered to, and they were not comprehensive enough.

1.3 The aims of the Rebus Symbol Development Project were to:

- · create a more consistent symbol set
- · reduce unnecessary visual clutter
- · provide a logical structure to the symbol schema
- · have symbols that would meet a greater linguistic need
- · be extendable
- · be appropriate for both direct and written communication

1.4 The structure of the project

The project was co-ordinated by Helen Whittle, working with Tina and Cate Detheridge at Widgit Software. The Rebus Symbol Development Project had at its heart a consultative group. This ensured that the changes to the symbol system and guidelines for new symbol production would be useful to a wide range of people. This group was made up of 23 individuals including speech and language therapists, educators, a psychologist and an AAC user. The project took the format of sending a series of questions to the group with a deadline. They were asked to answer the questions over a cup of coffee or in consultation with the symbol users they worked with. The replies were of a consistently high standard and were very detailed. All available space on the feed back forms were used to let us know what people thought of the symbols, and it was clear that there was significant consultation with users.

Initially the original symbols were examined closely to identify the key elements in the system, for example the 'question mark' or 'shop' symbol. Key elements and common design features were worked on first. The vocabulary was then considered in topics.

Some groups of symbols were easier to rethink than others, such as the symbols for shops and other buildings. Once a suitable key item had been found then the whole group of these symbols could be redrawn. These groups of symbols were the first to be put out to consultation. This was a good place for the project to start as in general it did not take too long to think about, and agreement could be reached quickly. In this way the consultation process became clear for all members of the group and the project produced some results fairly quickly.

As a result of this feedback new symbols were drawn and resubmitted for approval. Where there were no suggestions about alternative symbols from the consultation group or where there was no consensus a number of alternatives were drawn. These were sent out for further consultation. When these replies were returned the final decision about the content and format of the symbols was made from the consensus reached by the group.

At times there have been two clear viewpoints about a certain category of symbols and this has tended to be a split between those professionals working with people using symbols to develop literacy and those using symbols to support communication. This has in part lead to the development of alternative symbols for some concepts, and the creation of differentiated wordlists for use with different types of users. This is discussed in Section 1.6 to which references are made as appropriate.

1. 5 The revisions

There were many aspects to the symbol design that was considered. These ranged from technical considerations such as line thicknesses, through to the use of tones and colour to identify specific parts of a symbol. This section describes many of the decisions made and some of the rationale behind them.

Small buildings:
The generic item for building has been standardised, and has a floor. Normal buildings will have a single item in it.

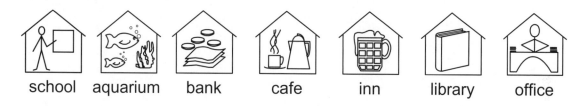

school   aquarium   bank   cafe   inn   library   office

Large buildings:
There is a new graphic to indicate large buildings, thus allowing a difference between similar buildings, e.g. clinic and hospital.

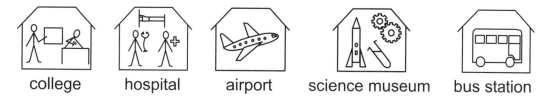

college   hospital   airport   science museum   bus station

Rooms:
A standard room element is a square.

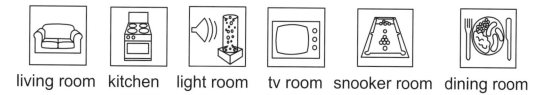

living room   kitchen   light room   tv room   snooker room   dining room

Small shops:
The standard shop is the building element plus the shop element in the roof. The type of shop will be represented by the smallest number of items possible, but certainly not more than 2.

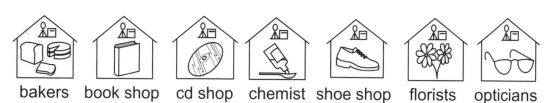

bakers   book shop   cd shop   chemist   shoe shop   florists   opticians

Large shops:
Large shops are distinguished by the large building element plus two shop elements.
Again this will have the smallest number of items, and not more than 3.

garden centre   supermarket   diy store

Businesses and organisations:
As well as buildings and shops there is a need to identify an organisation or business.
The concept of an arch will denote this. The arch plus coins (money) will distinguish a
commercial business from a non-commercial one. These can then be localised, for
example 'Car company' can be renamed using the F11 key to be Ford, or Avis.

NHS   RSPCA   Charity   Electricity company   Car company

Group:
Brackets are used to denote a group or subject (see education)

group   group   staff   committee

Categories:
A category is a group of three typical items.

plants   fat   animals   reptiles

Speak:
Speak uses the speech bubble rather than the wavy lines, (the wavy lines are also used
for heat). It is permitted to add content to the speech bubble where appropriate (as in
allow = say OK). Sound, however uses the speaker element. So animal sounds are not
represented by speech but by sound.

speak   advise   allow   speak up   ask   bark   miaow

Prepositions:
The positional item is in grey rather than black. The positioned element is the same size wherever appropriate.

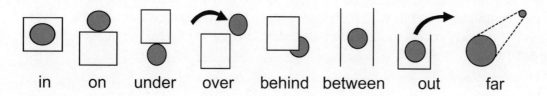

| in | on | under | over | behind | between | out | far |

Thumbs up/down:
A standardised thumb element is used in all cases. There is also an additional image for 'bad' in line with signing.

| good | readable | favourite | healthy | bad | bad |

Non pictorial elements:
Abstract symbols have always posed some problems, and it is questionable whether these are needed at the most basic symbol communication. However, where necessary, these have been maintained or redesigned along logical lines. It must be accepted that these symbols have to be learned.

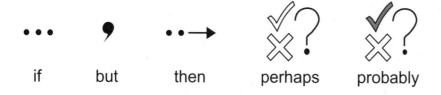

| if | but | then | perhaps | probably |

Arrows:
There are several different uses of arrows. These are standardised as follows:
1 A small straight arrow with small head for indicating (empty, bottom, every)
2 A thick arrow indicating movement direction (down, along, climb up, out)
3 A curved arrow with thin line for something happening ('change', and 'do' as "I am going to do the washing".

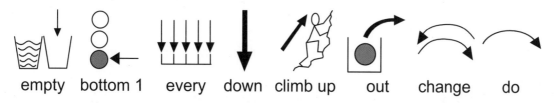

| empty | bottom 1 | every | down | climb up | out | change | do |

See the section on 'Make, Work and Do' for more discussion on this vocabulary.

Time:
A standard clock element with dots rather than numbers will be used in the main, but an alternative with numbers is used where this is of significance. There was much discussion about the use of hands on the clock. Having hands could imply a particular time, but not having hands made the element look either like a mat (without numbers) or a timer (with numbers). It was therefore decided by consensus that to have a time that was not quickly recognised, (seven minutes to two) would be the best compromise.

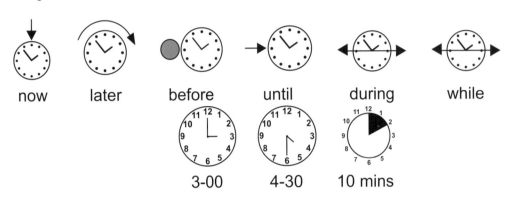

Days:
The days of the week are available with a coloured bar at the bottom. The use of colour is becoming popular as a reinforcement of the days of the week. A non-shaded option will also be available.

Negatives:
It was decided to introduce colour for negatives. These print well, with the colour element looking grey in print.

The 'not' element is standardised, but when used within a symbol only the diagonal line is used and not the circle. It is only intended to include common negatives and relevant contractions (don't, etc) . Others can be made with the two words.

Medical symbols:
The medical element of the green or open cross will be used with all medical items and people.

There was a need expressed to distinguish between doctor and nurse levels of practice. It was decided that a filled in cross would be used for the higher level and the open cross for the more general level (e.g. dentist and dental nurse). The group agreed that

6

at the first level users who may not discriminate between the colour and white cross, may also not appreciate the difference between the roles.

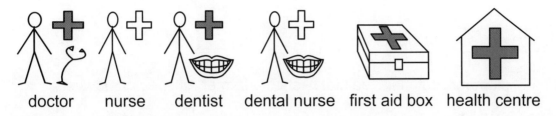

| doctor | nurse | dentist | dental nurse | first aid box | health centre |

Grey tone for emphasis:
There has been a lot of difficulty in previous use of an indicating arrow to draw attention to a certain part of a symbol. This has been replaced by the use of a grey fill or occasionally a thick line. In general thick lines work fine when the symbols are printed large, and reproduce quite well from a laser printer. However these do not show well on screen unless in large sizes. The fill is much clearer.

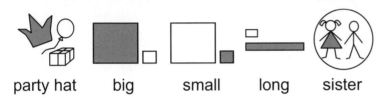

| party hat | big | small | long | sister |

Questions:
A standard question mark is used before an item to indicate a question. Many words are used in the English language to denote a question, and in these cases only the question mark is used: e.g. 'Do' as in "Do you like coffee?"

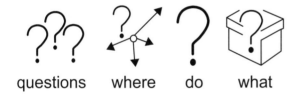

| questions | where | do | what |

Some questions may require a more concrete image. In the case of "where", for example, alternative symbols have been designed. Apart from the main question symbol, there is a more concrete symbol useful in more specific contexts. "Where" is also used in non-question contexts, for example: "This is where we live". This also requires a separate symbol.

| where | where | where |

People and Jobs:
People and jobs are represented by a person plus a relevant illustrative qualifier. There was much discussion on the order of these items. For example 'milkman' might, in the English language have milk first, man second. However, with 'painter' the order is less linguistically significant. The Speech and Language Therapists in the group felt strongly that the person should be first, as the most important element, which is then qualified.

After much consultation it was agreed to standardise on this approach (See also the section on plurals).

artist plumber butcher painter chef farmer inspector lawyer

Combined Words:
There has been a tendency to create unnecessary numbers of additional symbols where a concept is in fact represented by two words. The rule will be that where the two words used make a reasonable representation of the concept, then there should be no special symbol, for example 'hot food'. However where there is a single concept such as hair brush, frying pan, that will have its unique symbol.

strawberry jam   strawberry jam   strawberry   jam

The alternative styles are represented by the following structure:
-Example 1 has a single graphic with the strawberry as an integral element to the graphic.
-Example 2 is where the qualifying element for jam (i.e. strawberry) is shown with less prominence graphically, by making the combination with a qualifier.
-Example 3 is made from the two separate words.

Common items are made in style 1 but it is easy to create style 2 using the new Resource Manager. (Style 3 does not need creation).

Plurals:
There has been a lot of inconsistency in the illustration of plurals. Some irregular nouns have had their own symbols (e.g. mice) but others have not. There has been a plural qualifier available for some time, but it has not been greatly used. The use of the letter 's' has been rejected on two counts: we are trying to make an international symbol set and so letters are inappropriate. Also the addition of the letter 's' would be confusing in the case of irregular nouns such as mice.
There are three solutions offered:

1. The use of a qualifier.

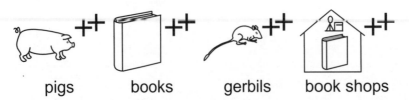

pigs   books   gerbils   book shops

2. In addition to the use of the qualifier for plurals with multiples of people, an alternative has been created with two people instead of one. This is because in some cases the plural qualifier can be confusing, for example when the symbol already contains an item such as the medical element (e.g. dental nurse).

lawyers   policemen   waiters   butchers   dental nurses

The program Writing with Symbols 2000 has a option to hide the plural qualifiers shown in example 1 above if preferred.

3. Some symbol users find the idea of plurals quite a difficult concept to grasp. A small number of basic nouns have been made into multiple image symbols to demonstrate the idea of plural. This is only suitable for images that are graphically simple.

apples   cars   dogs   cats

Comparatives:

Comparatives are only likely to be used at higher levels of vocabulary. Various alternatives have been tried, and the consensus suggests the following, using exclamations. One small one for the comparative and two for the superlative. The group consensus suggests that this works for users who can understand the idea of comparatives, and is ignored by others.

  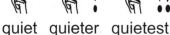

quiet quieter quietest   big   bigger   biggest

Tenses:

Tenses are dealt with in two ways depending on the tense. Simple past tense is represented by the arrow qualifier above the verb. In English the future tense is made with the single word 'will', although a set of symbols for the future tense will have the forward arrow above the image.

ran   ate   eating   runs   will   run   will   eat

The past perfect using the verbs 'to have' and 'to be' have been reconsidered. The use of the possessive 'have' image for a past tense (I have run) conveys an inappropriate image. Instead, there is an additional symbol of time (the clock) which carries the tense marker and the participle will not carry the tense marker.

| have eaten | have run | was cooking | were swimming |

Distance/size:

The grey shade is used to draw attention to the focus part of the symbol.

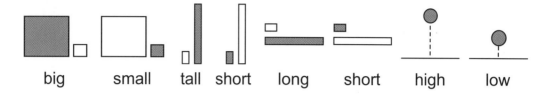

big   small   tall   short   long   short   high   low

Exclamation mark:

This is used for special emphasis

great   awful   easy   difficult   important

Family:

The circle continues to be used to indicate 'belonging'. Sister and brother are used with grey to draw attention to the target element, with a gender-less sibling in the circle. Family members from the wider family are represented by a circle with people in to indicate a man/woman/boy/girl related to the family. Step relations are indicated by a dashed circle.

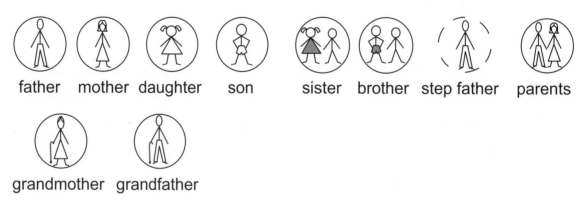

father   mother   daughter   son   sister   brother   step father   parents

grandmother   grandfather

wife   husband   boyfriend   girlfriend   partner

Other members of the extended family are indicated by an appropriate person with a 'my family group' element.

aunt   uncle   cousin

Do/work:
Do, Work and Make are used in various contexts. As well as a concrete sense, these words are often used to signify an abstract idea of action. The action element is a curved arrow signifying movement. e.g. ' I will do the washing up.' as opposed to the more concrete 'I will do that tomorrow.'

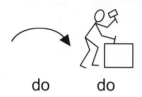

do   do

Similarly the concept of work has both concrete and abstract uses: 'I am working' (illustrating physical work or intellectual work) or the abstract 'Does the clock work?'

work   work   work

'Make' as in physical making is represented by a person making something, whilst the more abstract version is shown by an image of putting together two parts of a whole,

make   make

Ability or skill is shown by the abstract 'do' element plus the ticks for right ('do right')

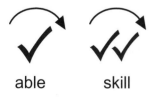

able   skill

Therapist:
The new image for therapist is based on the idea of helper with the 'helping hand'. A therapist is a special helper, and so has a star added to this. Therapy is the hand and star without the person.

helper therapy   therapist key worker

art therapy   speech therapy ·   speech therapist   speech therapy room

Learn:

After much debate it was decided to omit the pointing finger from the learn/think set of symbols. The original symbol emulated the sign, with the hand to the forehead. Users were offended by this (Paveley 1999) and the hand was moved to the chin to try to indicate somebody thinking. This has never been regarded as entirely satisfactory. The new symbol uses the think bubble with the face. An arrow in or out to show 'learn' or recall/remember and additional elements inside the bubble to qualify the meaning.

 learn   think   know   remember   clever   learning difficulty   explain

The most controversial symbol to develop is one for learning difficulty. The symbol illustrated here shows thinking with the 'difficult' element of the question mark and exclamation marks together.

Education:

These symbols are based on the original concept for 'teacher' as a person using a whiteboard to demonstrate/explain.

teach   teacher   class   classroom   lesson   education

Subjects are represented by the group element to denote the group of ideas on this topic, thus distinguishing between a globe and geography.

biology   maths   art lesson   history   geography lesson

The difference between a category and a subject may be seen by the example of tools and woodwork as a subject.

tools   woodwork

Hot and Cold:

A number of suggestions were considered. Heat seems to be universally acceptable as wavy heat lines, but images for cold were more difficult. The ideas most understood are wavy heat lines for heat, and snowflake for cold. However, in some parts of the world the snowflake is not such a good symbol (e.g. Australia) and the alternative zig-zag lines will also be available.

hot   hot chocolate   heater   hot   day

cold   fridge   cold   cold   hot

Non 'stick' people

Although the standard person is represented by a stick person, being genderless and non-cultural, there are times when a fuller figure is needed. This may be to allow emphasis, as in adult or child, or for certain actions, such as cuddle - which does not work with stick images.

adult   child   cuddle   friend   care

Faces

A more consistent approach has been taken to faces, especially when representing feelings.

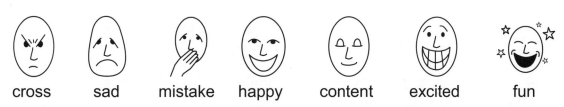

cross   sad   mistake   happy   content   excited   fun

Special
The star is used to indicate 'special'

special children   specialist   special plan   special offer

Pronouns
There are two types of pronouns illustrated. Personal and possessive:

The second person 'you' can be in either singular or plural. The plural as found by pressing the F12 key.

The third person can refer to either a person or an inanimate object. We have, therefore, added an inanimate alternative for both the standard and possessive pronoun.

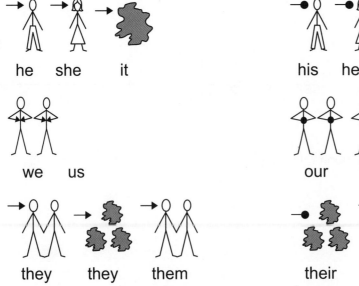

14

There is an additional symbol for 'me' that is more personal, since this is a very commonly used concept in this field, and it was felt that some users may be able to identify more easily with a more significant image.

me

Other countries and languages:
Writing with Symbols has been translated into several languages, with more in progress. There are flags for many different countries. Some symbols require alternatives for each country - for example the days of the week.

Thursday　　Jueves　　Donnerstag　　passport　passport　passport

There are also many culturally specific images now. These are normally included with the main vocabulary so that users can write about other cultures and geographical areas, e.g. Australia:

boomerang　bush ranger　crop dusting　didgeridoo　flying doctor　canopy

New vocabulary:
All of the vocabulary in the original Rebus Symbol Collection has been redrawn according to these conventions. A large number of duplicates have been removed and quite an extensive new vocabulary added.

New symbols include:

city 1　mobile phone　fax　pager　email　western　germs

national lottery　notebook　middle ages　egyptian　cattle grid　patience

1. 6 Using the new Widgit Rebus Symbol Collection

As well as redesigning and redrawing the symbols, other considerations had to be taken into account to ensure that the new symbols would be widely applicable. These issues include the structure of the wordlists and use of the symbols with languages other than English. Another key issue to be addressed concerns the care necessary in creating effective symbol supported materials.

Differentiated wordlists for use in Writing with Symbols 2000

Writing with Symbols 2000 uses a databse that links the text to graphic, called a wordlist. As well as having the range of alternatives for each graphic or word, described above, it is also possible to 'hide' symbols so that the F12 key has to be pressed to reveal it. This can be useful with abstract items and 'the' or 'a'.

>   **Level A** will have all items from the vocabulary. This will be provided both with and without explicit sex-education symbols.

>   **Level B** is aimed at young people and people who will be focusing on a basic communication vocabulary. The number of alternatives for any concept will be kept to a minimum, and complex items and grammatical markers will not be included. Some abstract words that may be used at this level will also be hidden.

Combined symbols versus one symbol per word

In the Rebus symbol set there were certain symbols that were used to represent more than 1 word e.g. "How much? " "Again please". In reviewing the set we have aimed to reduce this use of symbols to a minimum. Sometimes the combined word represents a unique concept that cannot be shown by two separate images, such as "wedding dress" and "life jacket" and a single image must be used. In other cases there is a greater correspondence between the indicidual words and the concept being expressed, such as 'Geography teacher' can sensibly be shown by two separate images.

Simplified language

However carefully the symbols are designed and however well they are taught, it is essential that the language level of the reader is recognised in sentence construction. The way the symbols are displayed can be crucial to the readability. The more concrete the vocabulary the easier it will be to illustrate the concepts graphically. Most punctuation marks are not shown in the graphic line and so the symbol reader will not easily see the ends of sentences, unless sentences are arranged on single lines. Long sentences with many symbols will be very difficult to interpret, whereas short sentences with few symbols may be much easier. Long sentences with few symbols will also be difficult to follow because the spacing between the symbols will not make sense graphically.

International Considerations

Writing with Symbols 2000 is currently being translated into a number of languages. The removal of the majority of text from the symbols has made the symbols more suitable for an international audience. Some symbols which represent cultural places or items may be of general interest when writing about other places and peoples.

These will gradually be added to the main vocabulary. There will also be some symbols which are very culturally specific, which will remain of interest only in each specific language or culture. These will be kept to a minimum.

Developing your own symbols in the Widgit Rebus style
These guidelines have been written to help explain the new ideas behind the symbols and to help with the construction of any new symbols in the future.

The utility program the Resource Manger, allows you to create your own 'portmanteau' symbols by combining elements. This is described more in chapter 2.

The conventions described should also allow you to create your own symbols using a drawing package, either starting from scratch or using elements from the drawings already published. An additional pack for symbol designers will be available with greater detail on the conventions and elements. If you do design new symbols using these guidelines or using the existing symbols, then we ask that you share your ideas so that they can be added into future upgrades. Access to large vocabularies will be increasingly important as symbol users begin to talk about wider topics and to participate more in society.

Chapter 2 Using the symbol glossary

2.1 The vocabulary

The Widgit Rebus Symbol Collection is a large and growing vocabulary with some 12,000 words illustrated. This glossary shows each image once, although in the program Writing with Symbols 2000 the same symbol can be associated with several words. Symbols can also be linked to qualifiers which add to the range of concepts covered.

(a) Words with more than one meaning
Many words have more than one meaning, and an important feature of the program Writing with Symbols 2000 is the way that it allows you to choose the most appropriate image for the meaning.

A pop   group.   A musical band or   group.   A   group   of objects.

A group of people.   The verb to group things

(b) Synonyms
Similarly there are many images that can be quite suitable for a range of synonyms:

for example: **lorry** is also linked to **articulated lorry, truck** and **HGV**

You can add your own synonyms easily in Writing with Symbols 2000, and add them to your own wordlists for further use. This allows you to personalise the symbol set to an individual's or organisation's particular vocabulary.

(c) Additional qualifiers
The Widgit Rebus Collection extends the meanings of the basic symbols with the addition of qualifiers. These are graphic indicators.

- Each verb is illustrated in the glossary in the present tense. In Writing with Symbols 2000 they are also given in the past tense with a past tense qualifier.
- Nouns are shown in the singular form, the plural form with the qualifier is given in the program. A small number of work people, are also illustrated in a plural form. These are shown in the glossary.
- Some adjectives are also supported by the comparative and superlative forms. In the majority of cases these extensions are created by using the main graphic and then adding a qualifier:

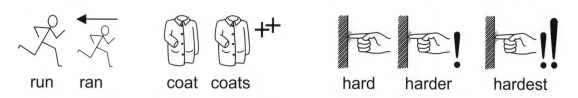

run   ran   coat   coats   hard   harder   hardest

Other vocabulary is created using different qualifiers of by combining more than one image:

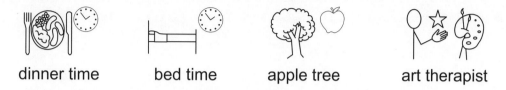

dinner time   bed time   apple tree   art therapist

You can use the Resource Manager, provided with Writing with Symbols 2000, to create your own combinations similar to those above, or to create entirely new concepts.

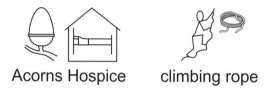

Acorns Hospice   climbing rope

2. 2 Symbols from different countries and cultures.

This dictionary indicates the symbols available in the English language set. It includes symbols from some other countries, not only for users in those countries but also so that users in one country can talk about places and items from other countries and cultures. This range and number of cultural symbols will increase in future updates.

2. 3 Using the Glossary.

The images in this dictionary are arranged in topics. Each image only appears once with one of the main definitions, although you will find many of the symbols linked to other words of similar meaning in Writing with Symbols 2000.

Many words could easily be classified under more than one heading - for example policeman could be classified under (a) People/workers, or under (b) Social and Community/Law and politics. When searching for a particular item you may find it useful to consider alternative main categories that could apply. The Contents list at the beginning of this book lists all of the main and sub-categories.

A few symbols use colour, however it is not possible to show these in this publication. The use of colours in the Widgit Rebus set are described in Chapter 1.

Chapter 3 - The glossary

1 PEOPLE

1.1 Family members

aunt

brother

brother

cousin

cousin

daughter

family

family

father

grandfather

grandmother

grandparents

husband

mother

nephew

niece

one parent family

parent

parents

partner

relative

single parent

single parent

sister

sister

son

step brother

step daughter

step sister

step son

stepfather

stepmother

uncle

wife

1.2 People: Pronouns

I — me — me — my

you — you — your

he — his — she — her

it — its

we — our

they — they — their — their

1.3 People: General

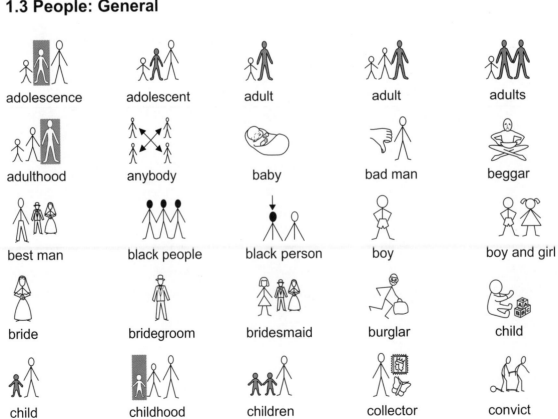

adolescence — adolescent — adult — adult — adults

adulthood — anybody — baby — bad man — beggar

best man — black people — black person — boy — boy and girl

bride — bridegroom — bridesmaid — burglar — child

child — childhood — children — collector — convict

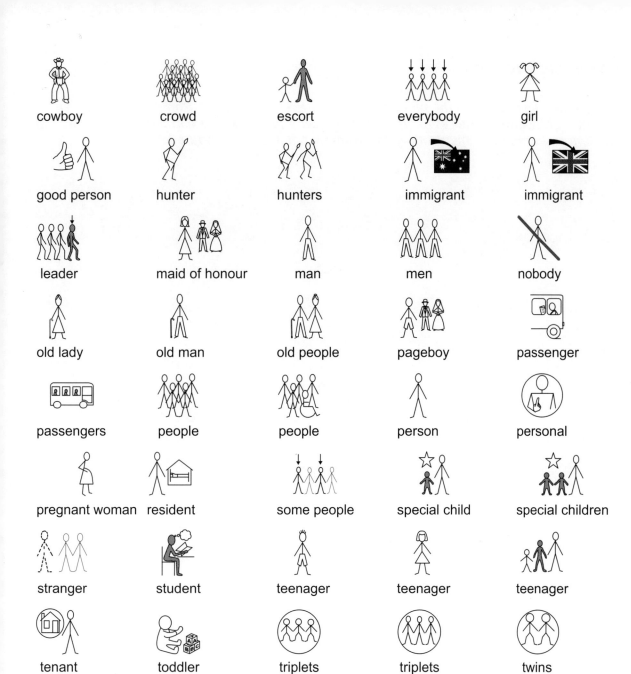

cowboy	crowd	escort	everybody	girl
good person	hunter	hunters	immigrant	immigrant
leader	maid of honour	man	men	nobody
old lady	old man	old people	pageboy	passenger
passengers	people	people	person	personal
pregnant woman	resident	some people	special child	special children
stranger	student	teenager	teenager	teenager
tenant	toddler	triplets	triplets	twins
twins	visitor	white person	woman	women

1.4 People: Workers Jobs

All people are included in the plural form with the plural qualifier. Some plurals also shown with multiple people. These are illustrated below. A few people are included under the topic heading rather than in this section, for example batsman and footballer.

artist	artists	astronaut	baker	bakers
ballerina	bank clerk	bank manager	bank managers	barber
barbers	barman	blacksmith	boss	boss
bricklayer	builder	bus conductor	bus conductors	bus driver
bus drivers	bush ranger	butcher	butchers	captain
captains	care manager	career adviser	caretaker	carpenter
carpenters	chef	chefs	cleaner	conductor
decorator	decorators	dental nurse	dental nurses	designer
drummer	dustman	dustmen	emergency manager	farmer
fireman	firemen	firewoman	firewomen	fisherman
gardener	government minister		greengrocer	greengrocers

grocer	guard	guitarist	hairdresser	hairdressers
head teacher	inspector	IT technician	IT technicians	jester
journalist	judge	king	lawyer	lawyers
learning support	librarian	librarians	lifeguard	lifeguard
lollipop lady	lollipop man	lord	lords	masseur
masseurs	mayor	member of parliament	milkman	minister
musician	musicians	painter	painters	pilot
pilots	plasterer	plasterers	plumber	policeman
policeman	policemen	policewoman	policewomen	porter
post woman	post women	postman	postmen	prince
princess	princess	queen	ring master	sailor
sailors	scientist	secretary	security guard	security guards

shop assistant	shop assistants	shop keeper	social worker	soldier
solicitor	solicitors	teacher	train driver	train drivers
train guard	train guards	treasurer	vet	vets
veterinary nurse	veterinary nurses	waiter	waiters	waitress
waitresses	welder	worker	writer	zookeeper

1.5 Friends, neighbours & social relations

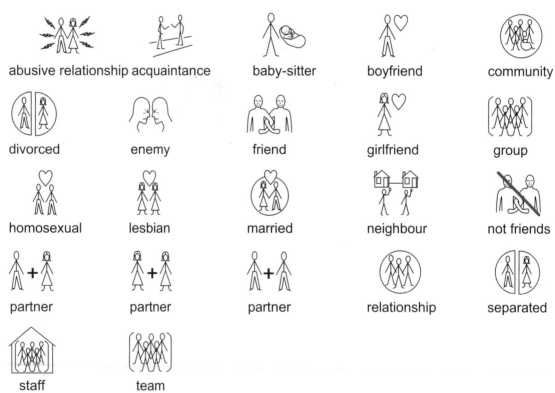

abusive relationship	acquaintance	baby-sitter	boyfriend	community
divorced	enemy	friend	girlfriend	group
homosexual	lesbian	married	neighbour	not friends
partner	partner	partner	relationship	separated
staff	team			

1.6 Fantasy or story characters

alien	fairy	genie	ghost	giant

26

gnome	Harry Potter	mermaid	monster	ogre
pirate	superman	tom thumb	werewolf	witch
wizard				

1.7 Specific people

David	Father christmas	Herod	sudhama

1.8 Nationalities

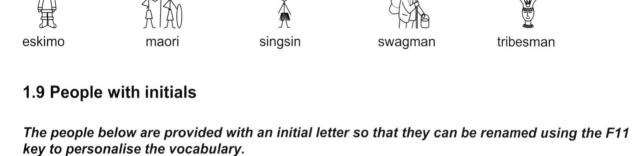

eskimo	maori	singsin	swagman	tribesman

1.9 People with initials

The people below are provided with an initial letter so that they can be renamed using the F11 key to personalise the vocabulary.

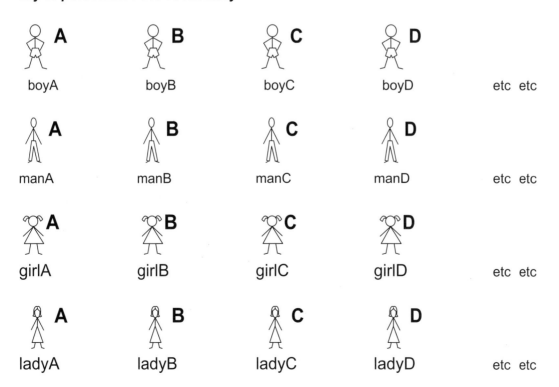

boyA	boyB	boyC	boyD	etc etc
manA	manB	manC	manD	etc etc
girlA	girlB	girlC	girlD	etc etc
ladyA	ladyB	ladyC	ladyD	etc etc

2 BODIES and PERSONAL CARE

2.1 Main body parts   *(more detailed body parts are listed under Biology)*

airways

ankle

arm

back

back

belly button

bladder

blood

body

body

body parts

bone

bones

bottom

bottom lip

brain

breast

breasts

calf

canine

cheek

cheeks

chest

chin

chin

ear

ear wax

elbow

eye

eyebrow

eyelash

eyelid

eyes

face

face

features

feet

finger

finger

fingernail

fingers

fist

foot

forearm

forehead

freckles

front

front teeth

gum

hair

hairy knees

hand

hands

head

heart

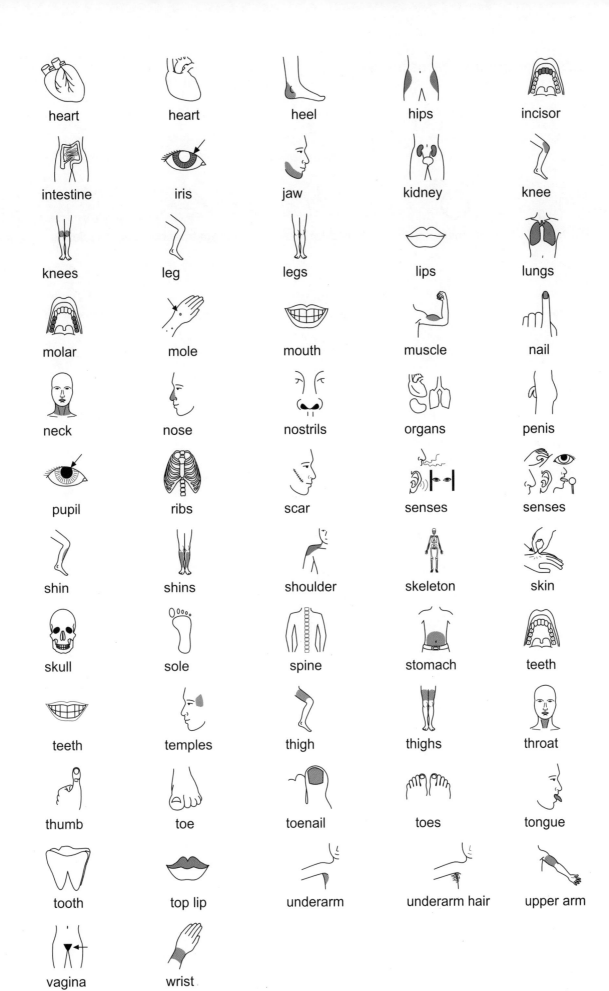

heart	heart	heel	hips	incisor
intestine	iris	jaw	kidney	knee
knees	leg	legs	lips	lungs
molar	mole	mouth	muscle	nail
neck	nose	nostrils	organs	penis
pupil	ribs	scar	senses	senses
shin	shins	shoulder	skeleton	skin
skull	sole	spine	stomach	teeth
teeth	temples	thigh	thighs	throat
thumb	toe	toenail	toes	tongue
tooth	top lip	underarm	underarm hair	upper arm
vagina	wrist			

2.2 Sex education vocabulary

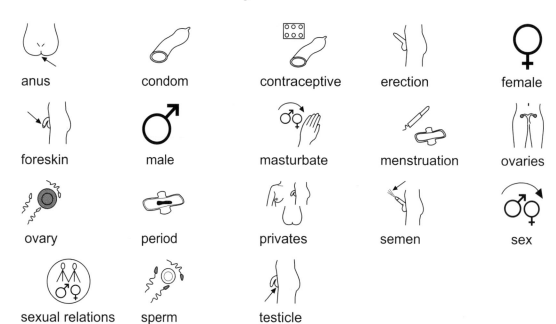

anus	condom	contraceptive	erection	female
foreskin	male	masturbate	menstruation	ovaries
ovary	period	privates	semen	sex
sexual relations	sperm	testicle		

2.3 Personal hygiene & grooming

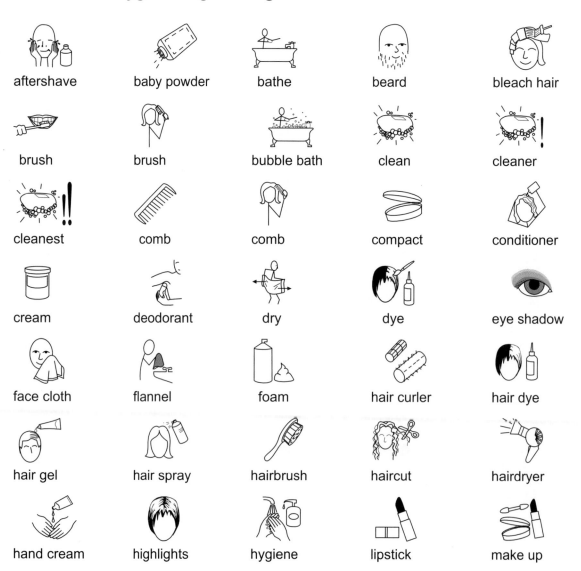

aftershave	baby powder	bathe	beard	bleach hair
brush	brush	bubble bath	clean	cleaner
cleanest	comb	comb	compact	conditioner
cream	deodorant	dry	dye	eye shadow
face cloth	flannel	foam	hair curler	hair dye
hair gel	hair spray	hairbrush	haircut	hairdryer
hand cream	highlights	hygiene	lipstick	make up

 make-up

 mascara

 moustache

 nail brush

 nail polish

 perfume

 perm

 razor

 sanitary towel

 shampoo

 shave

 shaver

 shaving foam

 shower

 soap

 soap dispenser

 sponge

 tampon

 tissues

 toiletries

 toothbrush

 toothpaste

 towel

 wash

 wash hands

 washing things

2.4 Description & states

 bald

 blind

 colour

 comfortable

 deaf

 disabilities

 drunk

 fat

 hearing impaired

 how old

 learning difficulty

 life

 middle age

 middle age

 new life

 old

 old

 partially sighted

 spotty

 strong

thin

young

young

2.5 Functions & actions

 birth

 breast feed

 blink

 blow nose

 breath

 breathe

 choke

 circulation

 cough

 cough

 dribble

 eyes closed

 faeces

 pulse

 pulse

 pulse

 saliva

 shaking

 shiver

 sneeze

 snot

 spit

 urine

 wind

 wink

3 MEDICINE and THERAPY

3.1 People

 art therapist

 audiologist

 audiologists

 chiropodist

 chiropodists

 chiropractor

 chiropractors

 dentist

 dentists

 dietician

 dieticians

 district nurse

 district nurses

 doctor

 doctors

 flying doctor

 GP

 GPs

 health and safety

 health officers

 homeopath

 homeopaths

 music therapist

 nurse

 nurse

 nurse

 nurses

 nurses

 nurses

 occupational therapist

 optician

 opticians

 osteopath

 osteopaths

 outpatient

 patient

 patient

 physiotherapist

 physiotherapist

 psychiatrist

 psychiatrists

 psychologist

 psychologists

 specialist

 specialists

 speech therapist

 speech therapist

 surgeon

 surgeons

 therapist

3.2 Medical & treatment places

  art therapy room

 clinic

 clinic

 dentists

fracture clinic

 GP's surgery

 health centre

 hospital

 hospital

 medical room

  music therapy room

 OT room

 opticians

 physio room

 plaster room

  speech therapy room

surgery

 therapy room

 vets

3.3 Equipment

 auroscope

 dental mirror

 equipment

 scalpel

 stethoscope

 stretcher

 syringe

  thermometer

 toning bed

urine bottle

3.4 Illnesses & medical problems

 addiction

 asthma

 backache

 bruise

 chicken pox

 cold

 cut

 dandruff

 drugs

 eczema

 epilepsy

 flu

 fracture

 german measles

 germs

 hangover

 headache

 hurt

hurt

ill

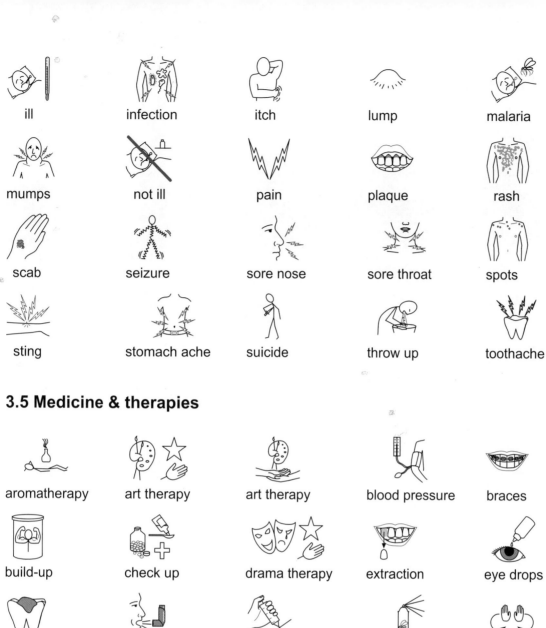

ill	infection	itch	lump	malaria
mumps	not ill	pain	plaque	rash
scab	seizure	sore nose	sore throat	spots
sting	stomach ache	suicide	throw up	toothache

3.5 Medicine & therapies

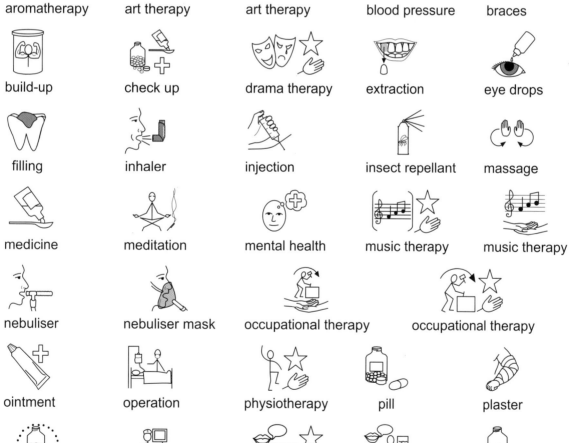

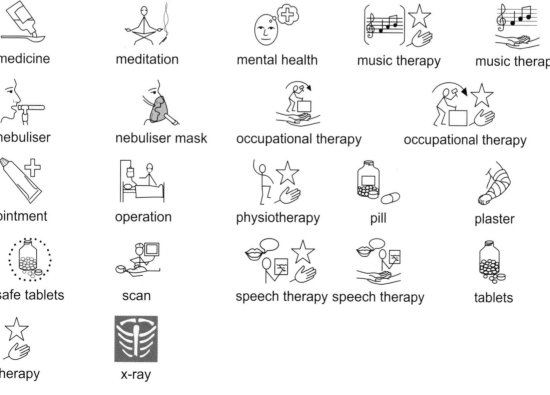

aromatherapy	art therapy	art therapy	blood pressure	braces
build-up	check up	drama therapy	extraction	eye drops
filling	inhaler	injection	insect repellant	massage
medicine	meditation	mental health	music therapy	music therapy
nebuliser	nebuliser mask	occupational therapy	occupational therapy	
ointment	operation	physiotherapy	pill	plaster
safe tablets	scan	speech therapy	speech therapy	tablets

therapy	x-ray

3.6 First aid

bandage

bandaging

cream

eyepatch

first aid

first aid

first aid box

plaster

sling

3.7 Aids & mobility

afo

clumper

crutches

electric wheelchair

foot rest

gaiter

grab bar

harness

hart walker

head rest

hoist

knee block

manual wheelchair

orthopaedic jacket

pool lift

radar key

ramp

ramp

robot feeder

rubber ferule

standing frame

support

turbo wheelchair

walking frame

walking stick

wheelchair

wheelchair track

3.8 Health

health

healthy

unhealthy

well

4 CLOTHES

4.1 General clothes

 anorak

 babygrow

 ballet shoe

 bikini

 blouse

 boot

 cagoule

 cap

 cardigan

 cloak

 clothes

 coat

 collar

 day clothes

 dress

 dressing up

 flipflops

 hood

 jacket

 jeans

 jumper

 kilt

 leg warmer

 leggings

 leotard

 mac

 over trousers

 pullover

 sandals

 sheepskin slippers

 shirt

 shoe

 shoes

 shorts

 skirt

 slippers

 sock

 suit

 sweat shirt

 t-shirt

 track suit

 trainer

 trainers

 trousers

 uniform

 waistcoat

 wellies

4.2 Underclothes

bra

dressing gown

knickers

night clothes

nightdress

pants

pants

petticoat

pyjamas

stockings

tights

underwear

vest

4.3 Special

apron

board shorts

dress up

Easter bonnet

grass skirt

overalls

police hat

police helmet

sarong

4.4 Accessories

anklet

backpack

baseball cap

belt

bib

bobble hat

bracelet

briefcase

brooch

buckle

button hole

coat hanger

contact lense

crown

ear ring

fan

glasses

glove

gloves

hair tie

hairband

hairclip

handbag

hanky

hat

hat

helmet

helmet

helmet

jewellery

 laces

 mask

 mitten

 necklace

 parasol

 pocket

 purse

 ring

 rucksack

 scarf

 strap

 sunglasses

 tie

 top hat

 umbrella

4.5 Parts of clothing & dressing

 button

 button hole

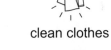 clean clothes

 change clothes

 dress

 fastenings

 put on

 shoe cleaning

 shoe heel

 sleeve

 take off

 velcro

 zip

5 EMOTIONS and ATTITUDES

5.1 Feelings

 afraid

 anger

 angry

 anxious

 bored

 confident

 confused

 content

 depressed

 depressed

 disappointed

 embarrassed

 excited

 frustrated

 happier

 happiest

 happy

 jealous

 lonely

 not frightened

 proud

 sad

 sadder

 saddest

 shy

 surprised

 unsafe

 upset

 very sad

 worry

5.2 Emotional states or actions

 awful

 brave

 comfortable

 cry

 dislike

 dislike

 dizzy

 do not agree

 don't love

 emotions

 enjoy

 favourite

 favourite

 feel good

 fierce

 frown

 great

 hate

 helpful

 homesick

 hurt feelings

 kind

 laugh

 lazy

like

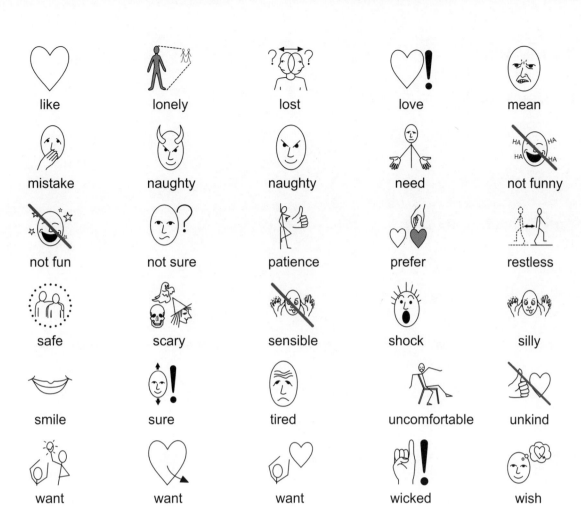

like	lonely	lost	love	mean
mistake	naughty	naughty	need	not funny
not fun	not sure	patience	prefer	restless
safe	scary	sensible	shock	silly
smile	sure	tired	uncomfortable	unkind
want	want	want	wicked	wish
wonderful				

5.3 Relationships & behaviours

argue	behaviour	belong	bully	bully
challenge	challenger	excuse me	in love	in love
manners	miss	pull faces	quarrel	regret

6 ANIMALS

6.1 Domestic & farm animals

calf	cat	cats	cattle dog	cow
dog	dogs	donkey	fierce	flock
flock	foal	gerbil	goat	guinea pig
hamster	herd	horse	kitten	lamb
mice	mouse	pets	pig	piglet
pony	puppy	rabbit	ram	sheep

6.2 Wild animals

anteater	badger	bandicoot	bat	bear
bilby	bull	camel	chimp	chimpanzee
cub	cuscus	deer	dingo	dormouse
echidna	elephant	elephant	fierce	fox
giraffe	gorilla	hare	hedgehog	hippo

kangaroo	koala	lemming	leopard	lion
llama	mammoth	monkey	ox	panda
platypus	possum	rat	reindeer	rhino
squirrel	stag	stoat	tasmanian tiger	tiger
wallaby	weasel	wild animal	wild pig	wolf
wombat	zebra			

6.3 Insects

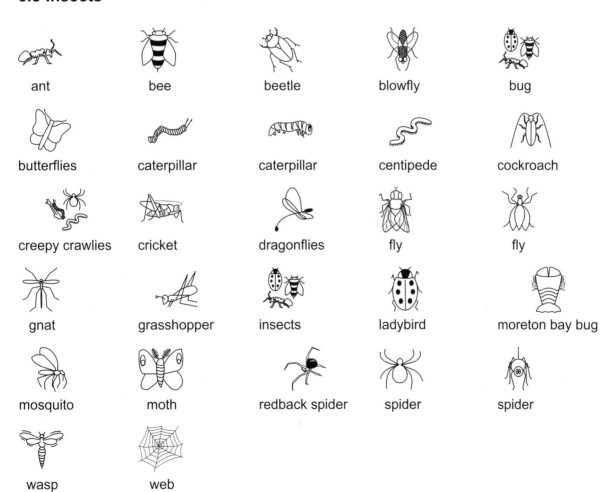

ant	bee	beetle	blowfly	bug
butterflies	caterpillar	caterpillar	centipede	cockroach
creepy crawlies	cricket	dragonflies	fly	fly
gnat	grasshopper	insects	ladybird	moreton bay bug
mosquito	moth	redback spider	spider	spider
wasp	web			

6.4 Aquatic creatures

blue ring octopus

cockle

crab

dolphin

dugong

fish

fish

goldfish

jellyfish

limpet

lobster

mussels

octopus

oyster

pond snail

prawn

sea anenome

sea horse

seal

shark

shell

shellfish

shells

shrimp

skate

starfish

tiddler

tropical fish

walrus

whale

whelk

winkles

6.5 Birds

bird

birds

black swan

blackbird

budgie

cockatoo

chick

chicken

cockerel

crow

crow

duck

emu

falcon

fledgling

galah

goose

hen

hornbill

kingfisher

kiwi	kookaburra	lyre bird	magpie	ostrich
owl	parrot	peacock	penguin	pigeon
puffin	robin	rook	seagull	sparrow
swallow	swan	thrush	toucan	turkey

6.6 Reptiles & Amphibians

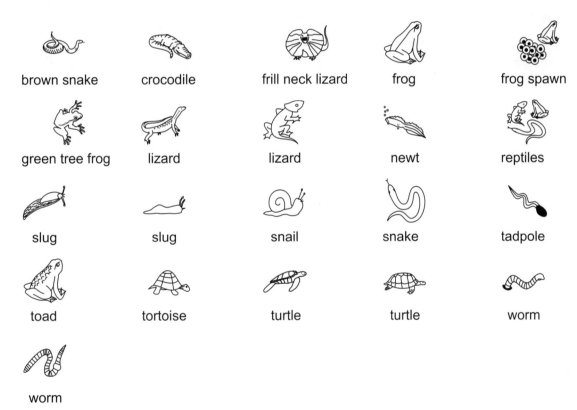

brown snake	crocodile	frill neck lizard	frog	frog spawn
green tree frog	lizard	lizard	newt	reptiles
slug	slug	snail	snake	tadpole
toad	tortoise	turtle	turtle	worm
worm				

6.7 General animal vocabulary

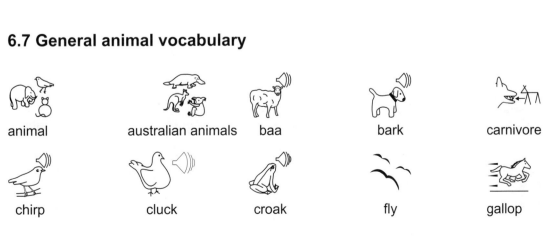

animal	australian animals	baa	bark	carnivore
chirp	cluck	croak	fly	gallop

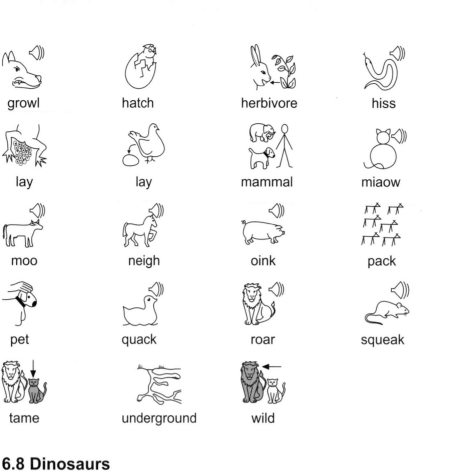

growl	hatch	herbivore	hiss	hoot
lay	lay	mammal	miaow	mini-beast
moo	neigh	oink	pack	pant
pet	quack	roar	squeak	stroke
tame	underground	wild		

6.8 Dinosaurs

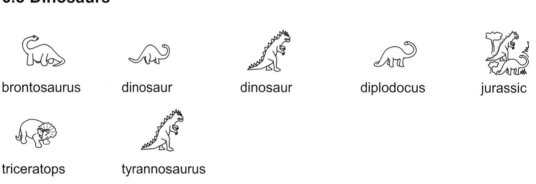

brontosaurus	dinosaur	dinosaur	diplodocus	jurassic
triceratops	tyrannosaurus			

6.9 Animal homes & places

animal home	animal hospital	aquarium	bird house	birdcage
burrow	butterfly farm	cage	cage	fish tank
goldfish bowl	hive	hutch	kennel	kennel
nest	pigsty	pigsty	sea life centre	stable

yard

6.10 Animal food

bird feeder

cat food

dog food

dry cat food

dry food

feed

feed

6.11 Animal body parts

animal hair

animal hide

antlers

beak

claw

fangs

feather

feelers

fins

fish bones

flipper

fur

gills

hoof

horns

mane

mane

paw

paw print

prickles

pupa

scales

shell

shell

skin

tail

trunk

tusk

udder

webbed foot

whiskers

wing

6.12 Animal equipment

animal bowl

animal equipment

bird table

collar

dog basket

grooming brush

lead

saddle

trap

trough

6.13 Fantasy animals

Blob

chompy

dragon

monkey king

rudolph

spikey

tor

7 ENVIRONMENT and NATURE

7.1 Flowers & plants

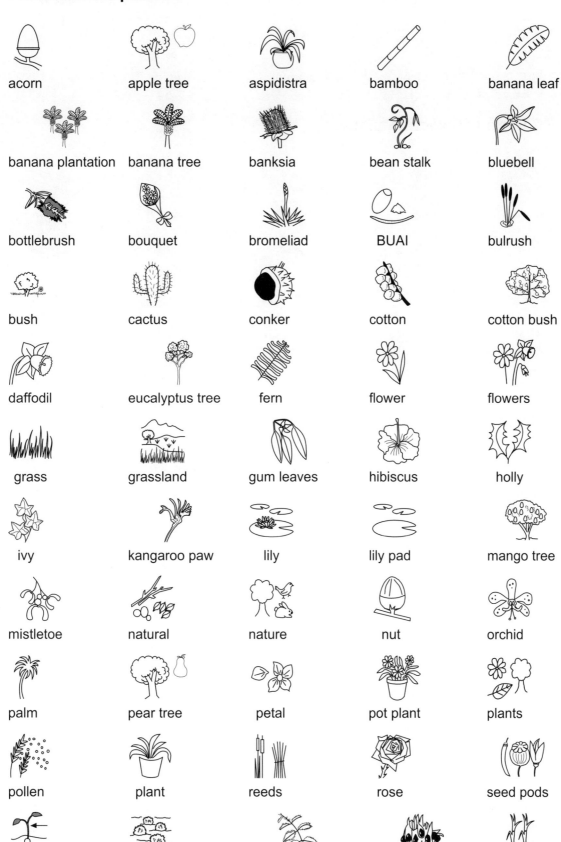

acorn

apple tree

aspidistra

bamboo

banana leaf

banana plantation

banana tree

banksia

bean stalk

bluebell

bottlebrush

bouquet

bromeliad

BUAI

bulrush

bush

cactus

conker

cotton

cotton bush

daffodil

eucalyptus tree

fern

flower

flowers

grass

grassland

gum leaves

hibiscus

holly

ivy

kangaroo paw

lily

lily pad

mango tree

mistletoe

natural

nature

nut

orchid

palm

pear tree

petal

pot plant

plants

pollen

plant

reeds

rose

seed pods

shoot

spinifex

stinging nettles

Sturt's desert pea

sugar cane

sunflower

 sycamore

 tea plant

 tree

 tree rings

 turf

 vine

 waratah

 wattle

7.2 Parts of flowers & plants

 branch

 bulb

 leaf

 leaves

 log

 plant

 root

 stem

 stick

 thorn

 timber

 tree trunk

 twig

7.3 Gardens, gardening & horticulture

 bone meal

 chop tree

 dig

 fence

 fertiliser

 flower bed

 fountain

 garden

 garden fork

 garden tools

 gardening

 gate

 germinate

 greenhouse

 hedge

 hoe

 lawn mower

 picnic table

 plant

 poly tunnel

 poly tunnel

 pot

 rake

 rake

 seedling

 seeds

 seeds

 shed

soil

spade

sow seeds
 sprinkler
 tropical house
 trowel
 water

 watering can
 well
 wheelbarrow

7.4 Farms & farming

 barn
 branding iron
 cattle grid
 cattle ranch
 cattle sale

 cotton farm
 crook
 crop
 crop dusting
 dairy farm

 dairy farm
 farm
 farm
 farm
 farm

 farmer
 farmer
 farming
 field
 hay

 hay
 haystack
 scarecrow
 shearer
 shepherd

 straw
 sugar cane field
 water tank
 wheat field

7.5 Countryside

 billabong
 bushfire
 bush fire
 canopy
 cave

 common
 country
 crater
 dam
 dam

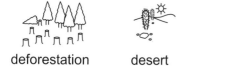 deforestation   desert   desert   earthquake
 environment

flood

 footpath

 forest

 forest fire

 geyser

 grassland

 ground

 Harvest Festival

 hill

 jungle

 lake

 landscape

 lava

 logging

 mountain

 mountain

 national park

 orchard

 path

 pond

 puddle

 pylon

 rain forest

 river

 river bank

 river walk

 stone

 stones

 stream

 turbines

 understory

 valley

 volcano

 volcano

 wall

 waterfall

 well

 wildlife

 windmill

 windmill

 windmill

 wishing well

 wood

7.6 Sea & Seaside

 bay

 beach

 cliff

 coral

 desert island

 docks

 harbour

 harbour building

 iceberg

 island

 island

 islands

 ocean

 pebble

 pebbles

pier

 port

 reef

 rockpool

 sand castle

 sea

 seaweed

 wave

7.7 Weather

 breeze

 change weather

 cloud

 cyclone

 dull

 fine weather

 fog

 gale

 hail

 hurricane

 lightning

 not raining

 rain

 rainbow

 sleet

 snow

 snowball

 snowflake

 snowman

 storm

 sun

 sunny

 thunder

 tornado

 weather

 windy

7.8 World

 air

 atmosphere

 earth

 earth

 equator

 ozone

 polar regions

7.9 Space

 earth

 galaxy

 galaxy

 Jupiter

 Mars

 Mercury

 moon

 Neptune

 orbit

 planets

 Pluto

 satellite

 Saturn

 sky

 southern cross

 space

 stars

 ufos

 universe

 Venus

7.10 Star signs

 aquarius

 aries

 cancer

 capricorn

 gemini

 leo

 libra

 pisces

 sagittarius

 scorpio

 taurus

 virgo

8 PLACES

8.1 Town & village

belisha

bollard

bridge

bridge

bridge

cemetery

city

city

county

crossing

crossing

high street

kerb

kingdom

lamp post

letter box

manhole

market

motorway

park

pavement

place

railings

road

street

telephone pole

terrace

town

traffic island

tunnel

village

village

village

walkway

zebra crossing

8.2 Park & zoo

bench

dinosaur park

fair

park

park

show ground

zoo

8.3 Specific UK places

Bristol

Blackpool

Channel Tunnel

dome

London

8.4 Specific Australian places

Ayers rock

ACT
Capital Territory

ACT
Capital Territory

NSW
New South Wales

NSW
New South Wales

NT
Northern Territory

NT
Northern Territory

nullabor plain

outback

Q
Queensland

Q
Queensland

SA
South Australia

SA
South Australia

Sydney

Sydney harbour

Sydney opera house

T
Tasmania

T
Tasmania

V
Victoria

V
Victoria

WA
Western Australia

WA
Western Australia

9 COUNTRIES

9.1 Flags

These are shown here in black and white as a guide to the country flags available.

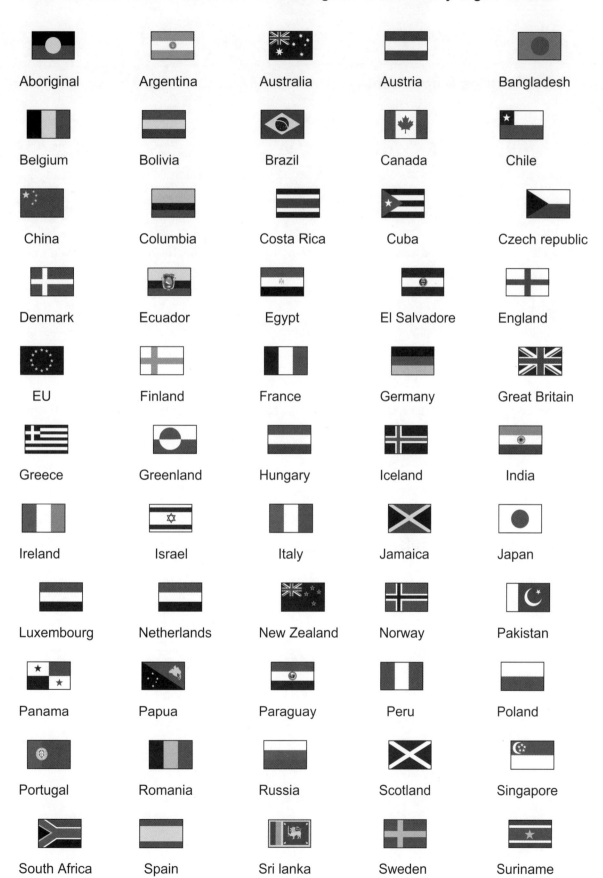

Aboriginal	Argentina	Australia	Austria	Bangladesh
Belgium	Bolivia	Brazil	Canada	Chile
China	Columbia	Costa Rica	Cuba	Czech republic
Denmark	Ecuador	Egypt	El Salvadore	England
EU	Finland	France	Germany	Great Britain
Greece	Greenland	Hungary	Iceland	India
Ireland	Israel	Italy	Jamaica	Japan
Luxembourg	Netherlands	New Zealand	Norway	Pakistan
Panama	Papua	Paraguay	Peru	Poland
Portugal	Romania	Russia	Scotland	Singapore
South Africa	Spain	Sri lanka	Sweden	Suriname

Switzerland

 Torres strait islands

Turkey

Ukraine

 Uraguay

 USA

 Venezuela

 Wales

9.2 Countries & continents

 Africa

 Africa

 America

 Antarctic

 Arctic

 Asia

 Australia

 Britain

 British Isles

 continents

 countries

 England

 Europe

 India

 Ireland

 New Zealand

 Northern Ireland

 Papua New Guinea

 scotland

 South America

 UK

 United States

wales

9.3 National vocabulary

Alternative images will be availble for each country for specific national vocabularies, for example passport, abroad, foreigner.

 abroad

 abroad

 abroad

 passport

 passport

 foreigner

 foreigner

10 SPORTS

10.1 Sports

 abseil

 aerobic

 AFL

 alpine skiing

 aquatics

 archery

 athletic

 badminton

 balloon

 basketball

 bike race

 bowling

 boxing

 bungy jump

 car race

 car racing

 caving

 crazy golf

 cricket

 cycle

 darts

 discus

 dive

 figure skating

 fishing

 football game

 gokart

 gokart race

 golf

 gymnastics

 high jump

 high wire

 hiking

 hockey

 ice hockey

 ice skating

 indoor athletics

 javelin

 jog

 judo

 karate

 long distance ride

 long distance run

 long jump

 martial art

 motorbike race

 mountain bike race

 netball

 orienteering

 outdoor activities

 parachuting

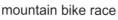 polevault

 pool

 quiddich

 quoits

 riding

 rodeo

 roller skating

 rounders

 rugby

 sailing

 sailing

 scuba

 shotput

skate

 ski

 ski race

 sledge

 snooker

speed skating

sport

 squash

 surf

 swim

table tennis

tennis

 thai chi

 trampoline

 triathlon

volleyball

waterski

  waterski

 weazeling

 weight lifting

wheelchair football

windsurfing

10.2 Sports people

 acrobat

 All Blacks

 archer

 athlete

 batsman

 bowler

 fielder

 fighters

 footballer

 referee

 rugby player

 sailor

 umpire

 wallabies

 weight lifter

 wicket keeper

10.3 Sports actions

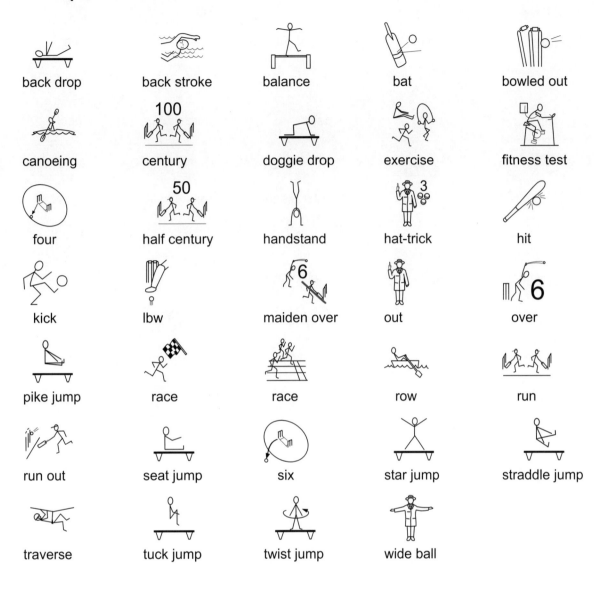

back drop	back stroke	balance	bat	bowled out
canoeing	century	doggie drop	exercise	fitness test
four	half century	handstand	hat-trick	hit
kick	lbw	maiden over	out	over
pike jump	race	race	row	run
run out	seat jump	six	star jump	straddle jump
traverse	tuck jump	twist jump	wide ball	

10.4 Sports equipment

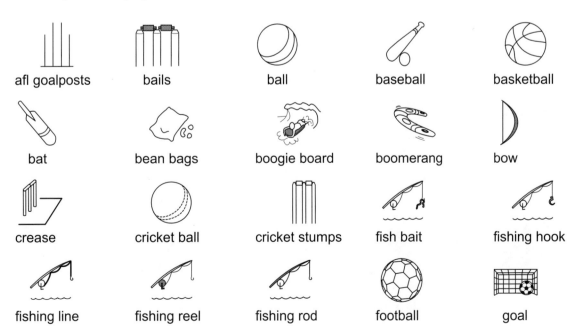

afl goalposts	bails	ball	baseball	basketball
bat	bean bags	boogie board	boomerang	bow
crease	cricket ball	cricket stumps	fish bait	fishing hook
fishing line	fishing reel	fishing rod	football	goal

goggles

 helmet

 life jacket

 net

 net

 oar

 paddle

pads

 parachute

pool

racing bike

racing car

roller blades

 roller skate

 rugby ball

rugby goal posts

sail

skateboard

 sledge

 snorkel

stop watch

swimsuit

target

trampoline

trunks

10.5 Sports places

 ballroom

 cricket pitch

 gym

 leisure centre

 riding school

 snooker room

 sports ground

 sports hall

 stadium

 swimming pool

 swimming pool

10.6 Sports events

 ashes

 horse race

 Melbourne Cup

 olympics

 one-day match

 special olympics

 tennis game

 test match

11 RECREATION

11.1 Hobbies & activities

act

activities

barn dance

beads

Boy Scout

Brownies

bushwalking

camera

collection

Cub Scouts

film

Girl Guides

hobbies

hobbies

leisure

leisure

line dancing

photo

photo album

photography

square dancing

11.2 Arts & crafts

arts

batik

canvas

cotton

craft

dummy

easel

frame

glass paint

glue stick

haberdashery

knit

knitting

knitting needle

knitting pattern

loom

model

model

monoprint

needle

paint

paintbrush

painting

paintings

paints

pin

pins

plaster cast

pottery

print

roller

 sculpture

 sew

 sewing machine

 silk screen

 sketchbook

 spray paint

 stick

 thimble

 thread

 weave

11.3 TV, film & hi-fi

 action film

 aerial

 animation

 Channel 1

 Channel 2

 button

 cartoon

 cassette

 cd case

 cd player

 change channel

 Channel 3

 Channel 4

 children's movie

 cinema

 comedy

 comedy

 comedy film

 drama

 dramatic movie

DVD
 DVD

 East enders

 eject

 fansasy movie

 fast forward

 film

 film

 headphones

 hi-fi

 horror film

 london's burning

 microphone

 pause

 personal stereo

 play

 programme

 projector

 radio

 record

 record

 record player

 remote control

 rewind

 romantic movie

 sci-fi movie

screen

 speaker

 speakers

 stereo

 tape

 tele-video

 television

 the bill

 VCR

 western

11.4 Recreational places

 ball pool

 club

 leisure centre

 leisure centre

 play room

 playground

playgroup

toy library

11.5 Toys & games

 balloon

 board game

 bouncy castle

 bricks

 bubble tube

 cards

 catapult

 chess

 chess

 climbing frame

 clubs

 coconut shy

 diamonds

 dice

 dice·

 doll

 domino

 duplo

 game

 games

 games console

 glove puppet

 glow ball

 glow wand

 hearts

 hoop

 hopscotch

 i-spy

 jack

 jack-in-the-box

 juggle

 king

 kite

 lego

 marble

messy play

 multilink

 parachute game

 party game

 Patience

 play

 play

 play a game

 play cards

 playdough

 playhouse

 puppet

 puzzle

 queen

 rattle

 robot

 rocking horse

 roundabout

 sand pit

 sandpit

 seesaw

 seesaw

 skip

 skipping rope

 slide

 slinky

 softplay

 solitaire

 spades

 swing

 swing

 teddy

 toy

 toy car

 toy sack

 toy train

 train set

 video game

 waterplay

11.6 Music

 accordion

 band

 band

 bell

 bells

 carol

 castanets

 cellist

 cellists

 cello

 chimebar

 choir

 classical music

 cymbal

 dance music

 didgeridoo

 disco

 double bass

 drum

 guitar

harp

 hum

 instruments

 karaoke

 keyboard

 kundu

 line dancing

 maracas

 military music

 music

 music stand

 opera

 orchestra

 organ

 peal

 percussion

 percussionist

 percussionists

 pianist

 pianists

 piano

 piano

 pipe music

 pipes

 play keyboard

 record

 rhythm

 samba

 saxophone

 shaker

 sing

 song

 strings

 tambourine

 timpani

 trombone

 trombonist

 trombonists

 trumpet

 trumpet

 trumpeter

 trumpeters

 violin

 violinist

 violinists

 whistle

 xylophone

11.7 Entertainments & entertainers

 audience

 big dipper

 big top

 big wheel

 big wheel

 clown

 circus

 circus ring

 concert

 dance theatre

dodgems

 entertain

 firework

 fun

 gladiator

 helter skelter

 magic

 magician

 magicians

 merry-go-round

 musical

 pantomime

 performing arts

 play

 play

 puppet show

 scenery

 sideshow

 sparkler

stage

 stage

 stage light

theatre

11.8 Holidays & holiday items

 adventure

 bank holiday

 beach bag

 beach towel

 beach umbrella

 camp

 camp fire

 day off

 holiday

 lilo

 luggage

 pack

 school holiday

 suitcase

 sun cream

 tent

12 ACTIONS

Verbs are available with present and past tenses.
Please see the discussion in section 1 on the different past tenses

12.1 Actions & adverbs involving people

approach	assemble	become	begin	bring
burn	carry	catch	catch	chase
climb	climb down	climb up	climb tree	climb tree
crawl	creep	dance	do	drop
fall	fight	find	find	follow
force	gather	get	get	give
grow	grow up	hang	help	help
help	hide	hide	hop	hunt
hurry	ignore	join	jump	jump off
jump over	jump up	kill	kneel	leave
lie	lie down	lift	live	look at

make	meet	miss	mobility	move
move house	pay attention	pick up	poke	prevent
pull	punch	push	push	put away
queue	ramble	reach	receive	relax
rescue	run	scratch	scrub	see
shake	should	sit	sit down	skip
sleep	slip	smack	smell	smoke
sniff	stamp	stand	stand up	stare
start	stay	stay	stay at	steal
steal	step	stomp	take	take
take	throw	tickle	tidy	tip
touch	treat	trip	try	try harder

try hardest	turn	visit	wait	wake up
walk	win	wipe	work	work
work hard	work hard	wring		

12.2 General actions & adverbs

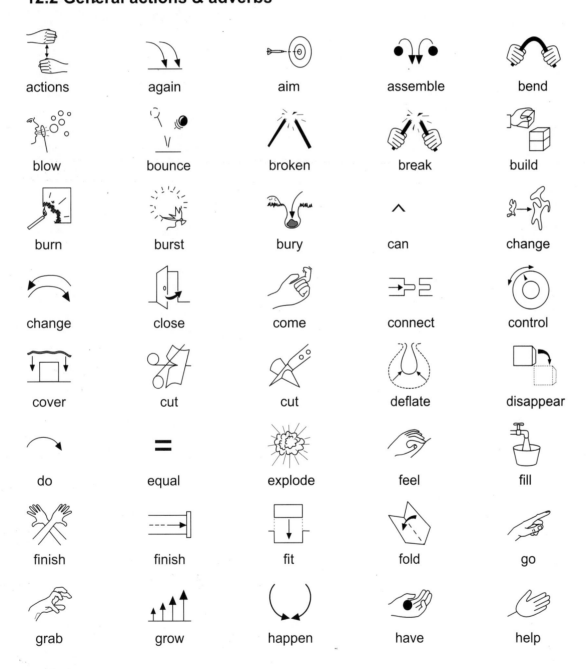

actions	again	aim	assemble	bend
blow	bounce	broken	break	build
burn	burst	bury	can	change
change	close	come	connect	control
cover	cut	cut	deflate	disappear
do	equal	explode	feel	fill
finish	finish	fit	fold	go
grab	grow	happen	have	help

hit	hold	inflate	is	keep
knock	knock down	let go	light	lock
magnify	magnify	make	match	melt
mend	move	muddle	muffle	open
open	pick	pinch	poke	prepare
press	pressure	protect	pull	put
recycle	replace	reverse	roll	rub
separate	sequence	shake	share	slide
sort	spill	spin	splash	squash
squeeze	squirt	start	stir	stop
store	stretch	swing	switch off	switch on
tear	tidy	tie	turn	use

wind

work

12.3 Negatives

can't

can't come

can't   feel

can't find

can't   see

didn't

don't touch

don't

don't

don't go

don't have

don't pull

don't push

don't touch

don't want

don't want

don't want

isn't

No smoking

not working

not working

13 DIRECTION & POSITION

13.1 Direction

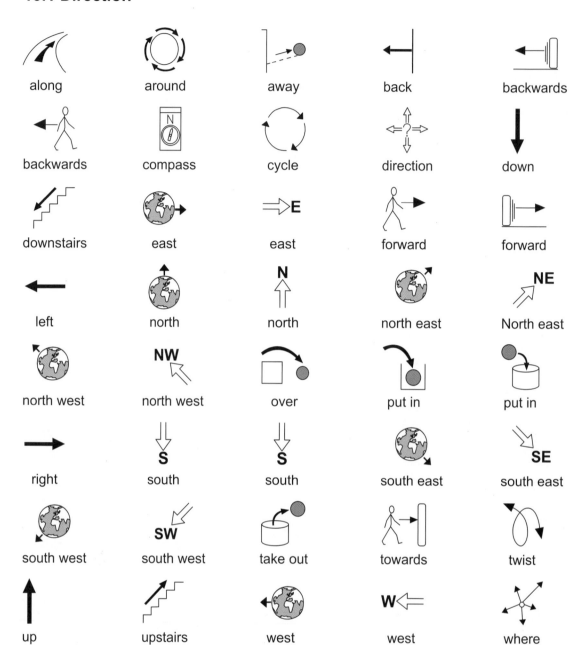

13.2 Position

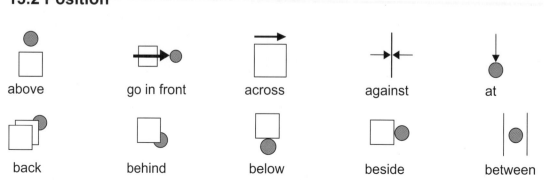

beyond | bottom | bottom | everywhere | from
front | go behind | go under | here | in
in front | inside | into | low | lower
lowest | middle | middle | not here | nowhere
off | on | onto | out | outdoors
outdoors | outside | position | side | somewhere
there | there is | through | to | together
top | top | touch | under | upside down

13.3 Relative positions

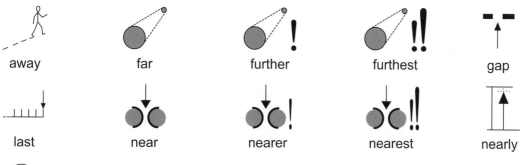

away | far | further | furthest | gap
last | near | nearer | nearest | nearly

next

14 TIME and DATES

14. 1 Comparative

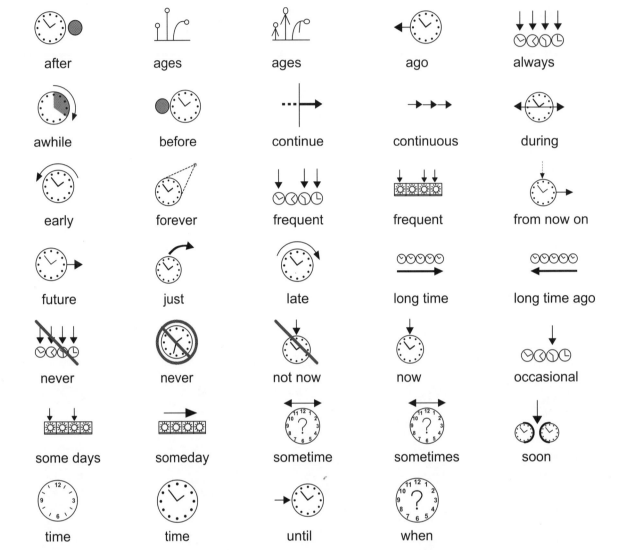

after	ages	ages	ago	always
awhile	before	continue	continuous	during
early	forever	frequent	frequent	from now on
future	just	late	long time	long time ago
never	never	not now	now	occasional
some days	someday	sometime	sometimes	soon
time	time	until	when	

14.2 Units of time

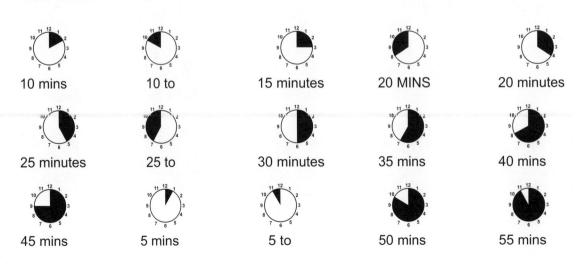

10 mins	10 to	15 minutes	20 MINS	20 minutes
25 minutes	25 to	30 minutes	35 mins	40 mins
45 mins	5 mins	5 to	50 mins	55 mins

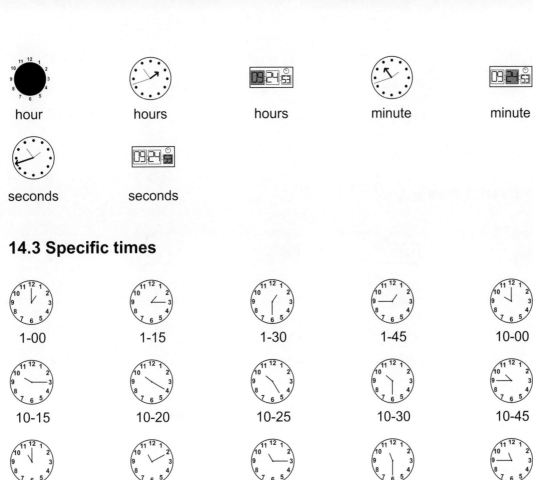

hour   hours   hours   minute   minute

seconds   seconds

14.3 Specific times

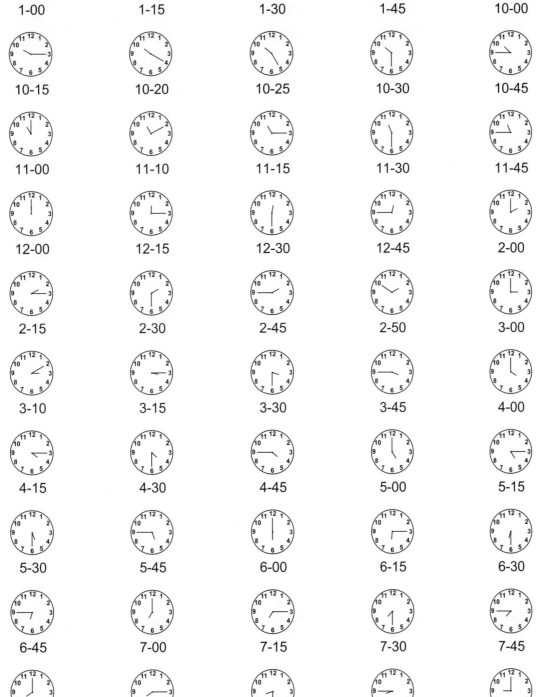

1-00	1-15	1-30	1-45	10-00
10-15	10-20	10-25	10-30	10-45
11-00	11-10	11-15	11-30	11-45
12-00	12-15	12-30	12-45	2-00
2-15	2-30	2-45	2-50	3-00
3-10	3-15	3-30	3-45	4-00
4-15	4-30	4-45	5-00	5-15
5-30	5-45	6-00	6-15	6-30
6-45	7-00	7-15	7-30	7-45
8-00	8-15	8-30	8-45	9-00

9-15   9-30   9-45

14.4 Event times

 anniversary   anniversary   anniversary   anniversary   appointment

 bed time   dinner time   free time   home time   interval

 lunch time   play time   school time   story time

14.5 Days & months

 one day   day   morning   afternoon   evening

 night   yesterday   tomorrow   last night   tomorrow night

 tonight   today   good afternoon   good day   good evening

 good morning   good night   everyday   week   week

 weekend   weekend   weekend   last week   last week

 next week   next week   month   month   last month

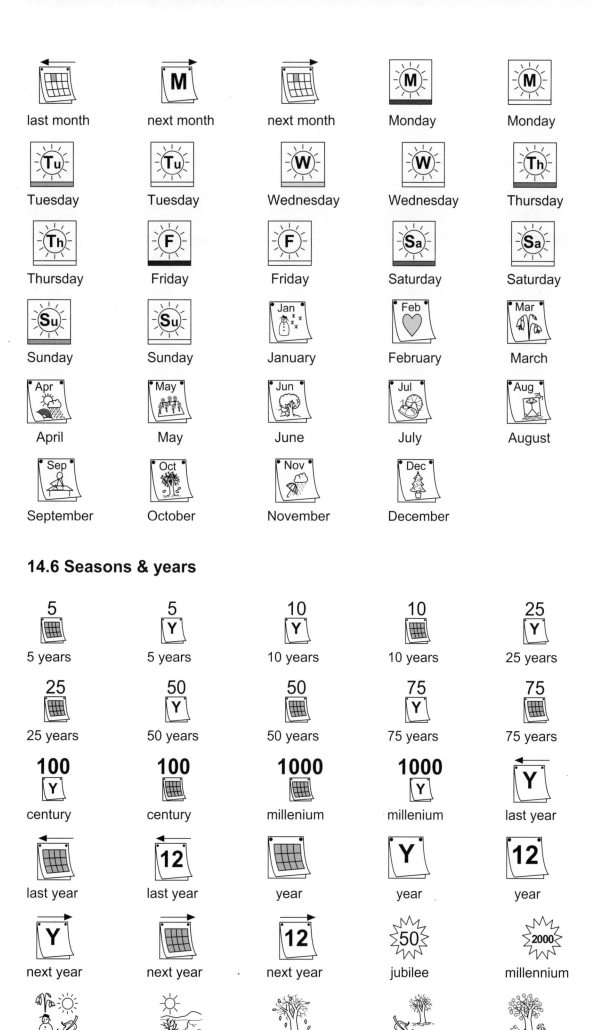

last month   next month   next month   Monday   Monday

Tuesday   Tuesday   Wednesday   Wednesday   Thursday

Thursday   Friday   Friday   Saturday   Saturday

Sunday   Sunday   January   February   March

April   May   June   July   August

September   October   November   December

14.6 Seasons & years

5 years   5 years   10 years   10 years   25 years

25 years   50 years   50 years   75 years   75 years

century   century   millenium   millenium   last year

last year   last year   year   year   year

next year   next year   next year   jubilee   millennium

seasons   dry season   autumn   autumn   spring

spring

 summer

 summer

 wet season

 winter

 winter

 year

1946

1946

1997

1997

1998

1998

1999

1999

14.7 Specific days

 Anzac day

 Australia day

 bonfire night

 boxing day

 Christmas Day

 Easter Sunday

 Good Friday

 halloween

 halloween

 holiday

 pancake day

 special day

14.8 Devices

 alarm clock

 calendar

 calendar

 clock

 clock face

 timer

 timetable

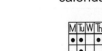 timetable

 watch

 watch

15 SIZE

15.1 Number & units

0	**1**	**2**	**3**	**4**
0	1	2	3	4

through to . . . .

96	**97**	**98**	**99**	**100**
96	97	98	99	100

2000	**2001**		**2009**	**2010**
2000	2001	**through to . . . .**	2009	2010

1 lb	100g	100g	2 tablespoons	2 teaspoons
3 teaspoons	4th	500g	50g	50g
5kg	5th	first	centimeter	gram
half	half	half	half cup	kg
kg	lb	litre	metre	millimetre
number	ordinal number	ounce	pint	quarter
quarter	second	third		

81

15.2 Size & quantity

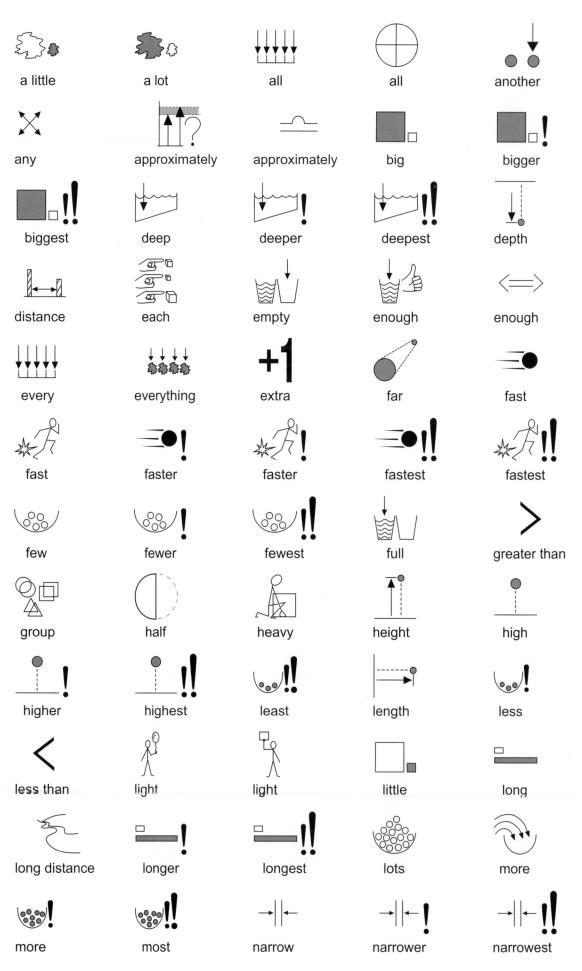

a little	a lot	all	all	another
any	approximately	approximately	big	bigger
biggest	deep	deeper	deepest	depth
distance	each	empty	enough	enough
every	everything	extra	far	fast
fast	faster	faster	fastest	fastest
few	fewer	fewest	full	greater than
group	half	heavy	height	high
higher	highest	least	length	less
less than	light	light	little	long
long distance	longer	longest	lots	more
more	most	narrow	narrower	narrowest

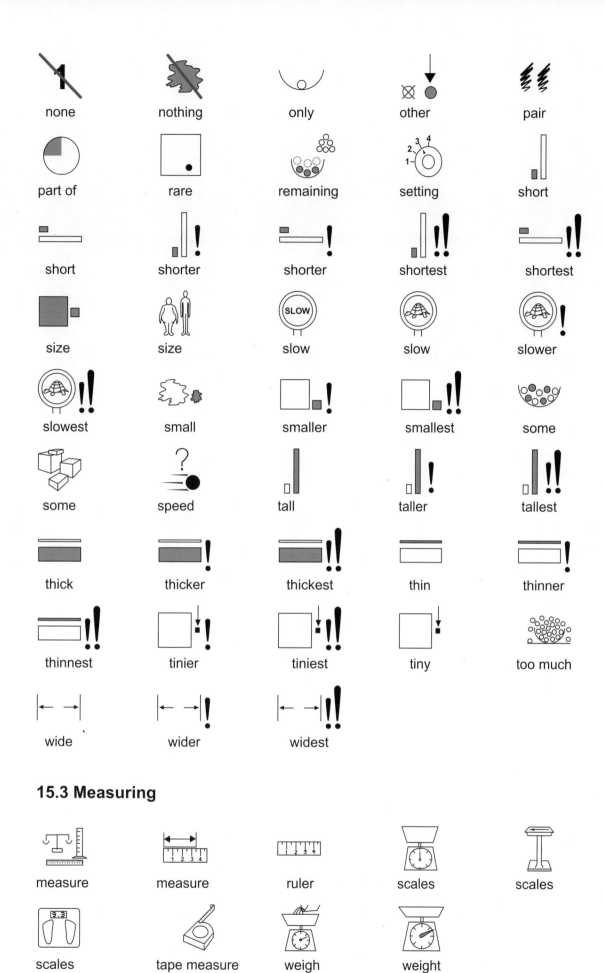

nothing

only

other

pair

part of

rare

remaining

setting

short

short

shorter

shorter

shortest

shortest

size

size

slow

slow

slower

slowest

small

smaller

smallest

some

some

speed

tall

taller

tallest

thick

thicker

thickest

thin

thinner

thinnest

tinier

tiniest

tiny

too much

wide

wider

widest

15.3 Measuring

measure

measure

ruler

scales

scales

scales

tape measure

weigh

weight

16 SHAPE

16.1 Shapes

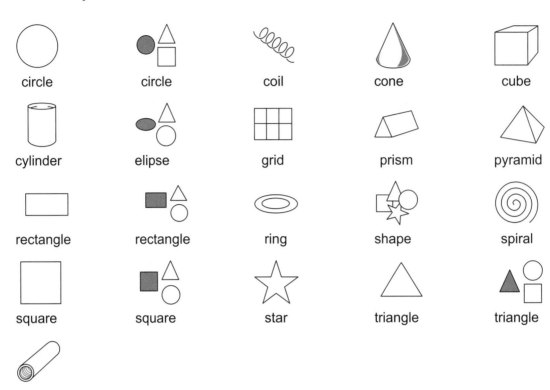

circle	circle	coil	cone	cube
cylinder	elipse	grid	prism	pyramid
rectangle	rectangle	ring	shape	spiral
square	square	star	triangle	triangle
tube				

16.2 Properties

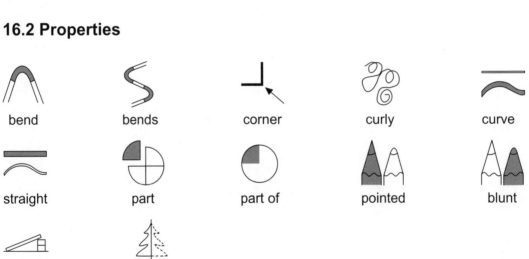

bend	bends	corner	curly	curve
straight	part	part of	pointed	blunt
slope	symmetry			

17 COLOUR & APPEARANCE

17.1 Colour names

There are coloured shapes for each of the following:

black	brown	dark blue	gold	green
grey	indigo	light green	orange	pink
purple	red	silver	violet	white
yellow				

17.2 Descriptions

appearance

beautiful

bright

brighter

brightest

camouflage

checks

colours

cute

dark

dark

different

dim

dull

handsome

light

not handsome

opposite

pattern

patterned

plain

pretty

reflection

same

shade

shade

shadow

shiny

smart

smart

spotted

straight

stripes

tartan

ugly

very different

85

18 MATERIALS and THEIR PROPERTIES

18.1 Materials

 aluminium

 bleach

 cardboard

 cement

 ceramic

 chalk

 china

 clay

 cloth

 coal

 flint

 frankincense

 gas

 gas

 gas

 glass

 glue

 glue

 gold

 gold

 granite

 grit

 ice

 ice cube

 leather

 limestone

 liquid

 material

 mesh

 metal

  mould

 mud

 myrrh

 oxygen

 paper

 paste

 plank

 plastic

 plasticine

 poison

 polystyrene

 rock

 rubber

 sand

 silk

 silver

 silver metal

 smoke

 steam

 water

  water

 wood

 wool

 woollen

18.2 Properties or features of materials

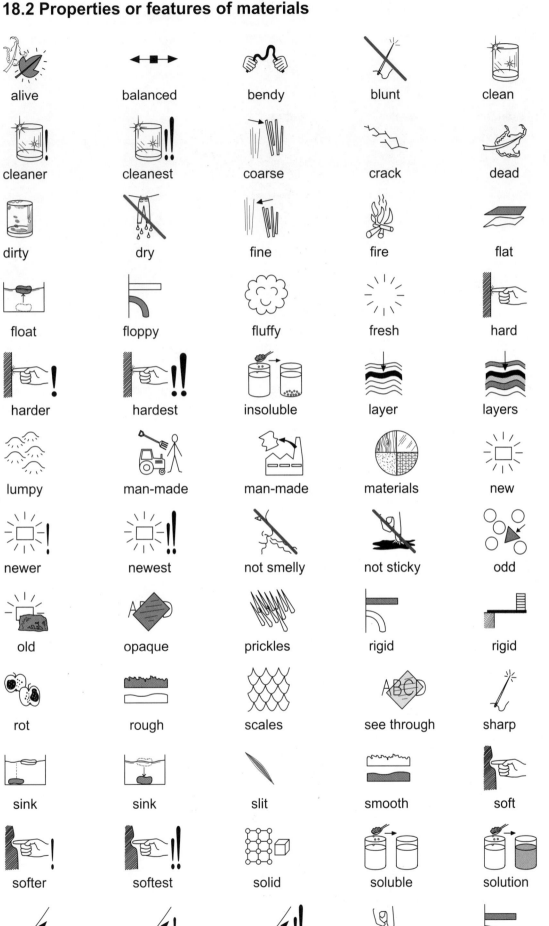

alive	balanced	bendy	blunt	clean
cleaner	cleanest	coarse	crack	dead
dirty	dry	fine	fire	flat
float	floppy	fluffy	fresh	hard
harder	hardest	insoluble	layer	layers
lumpy	man-made	man-made	materials	new
newer	newest	not smelly	not sticky	odd
old	opaque	prickles	rigid	rigid
rot	rough	scales	see through	sharp
sink	sink	slit	smooth	soft
softer	softest	solid	soluble	solution
steep	steeper	steepest	sticky	stiff

still

strong

suspension

tacky

translucent

unbalanced

weak

wet

19 SOUND AND TEMPERATURE

19.1 Sound

echo

how loud

loud

louder

loudest

noise

not quiet

quiet

quiet place

quieter

quietest

sound

whistle

19.2 Temperature

boiling point

cold

cold

cold

colder

coldest

freeze

freezing point

hot

hot

hot

hotter

hottest

temperature

temperature

warm

89

20 FOOD and DRINK

20.1 Drinks

alcohol	apple juice	apricot juice	Baileys	beer
beer can	beer cans	blackcurrant juice	blackcurrant squash	
box drink	brandy	can	cappuccino	cherry juice
chocolate milk	cider	cocktail	coffee	coffee
coffeebeans	drink	drinks	fizzy	fizzy drink
grape juice	hot chocolate	juice	juice	lager
lemon juice	lemonade	lime juice	milk	milk
milk shake	orange juice	peach juice	pear juice	pineapple juice
raspberry juice	red wine	squash	strawberry juice	tea
tea and coffee	tea bag	tomato juice	tonic water	whisky
white wine	wine			

20.2 Fruit & vegetables

 almonds

 apple

 apples

 apricot

 asparagus

 aubergine

 avocado

 baby corn

 banana

 bananas

 beans

 beans

 beansprouts

 beetroot

 berries

 berry

 blackcurrant

 broccoli

 cabbage

 carrot

 cauliflower

 celery

 cherry

 chestnut

 coconut

 core

 corn

 courgette

 cucumber

 currants

 dates

 fruit

 garlic

 gooseberry

 grape

 grapefruit

 grapes

 guava

 hazelnut

 kiwi fruit

 leek

 lemon

 lettuce

 lime

 mange tout

 mango

 marrow

 mushroom

 olive

 olives

 onion

 orange

 oranges

 parsnip

 passion fruit

 pawpaw

 peach

 peanut

 pear

 pears

peas

 pepper

 pineapple

 plum

 potato

 potatoes

 prunes

 radish

 raisins

 raspberry

 rhubarb

 rice

 salad

 satsuma

 silver beet

 spinach

 spring onion

 sprouts

 strawberries

 strawberry

 swede

 tangerine

 tomato

 turnip

 vegetables

 vegetables

 watermelon

20.3 Meat & fish

 bacon

 beef

 beefburger

 chicken

 chicken nugget

 fish fingers

 haggis

 ham

 hot dog

 kebab

 lamb

 meat

 meat

 pate

 pork chop

 poultry

 sausage

 sausage

 sausage roll

 steak

 tinned fish

20.4 General foods & dairy foods

apricot jam	bagel	baking powder	bap	barley
beans	blackcurrant jam	boiled egg	bran	bread
bread crumbs	bun	butter	carbohydrate	chapatti
cheese	cheese	cherry jam	chips	chocolate spread
cream	croissant	crumpet	dairy foods	egg
eggs	fat	filling	flan	flour
flour	food	fried egg	grains	honey
hot food	ingredients	jam	lemon curd	lentils
macaroni	margarine	marmalade	marmite	mashed potato
mince	muesli	naan	noodles	oats
oil	olive oil	omelette	pasta	peach jam
peanut butter	Pediasure	pie	pie	plum jam

porridge
 protein
 raspberry jam
 roll
 rye

 soup
 strawberry jam
 sugar
 sugar puffs
 tart

 toast
 vegemite
 vegetarian
 weetabix
 wheat

20.5 Savory foods & meals

 beans on toast
 bolognaise
 breakfast
 breakfast
 burger

 continental breakfast
 curry
 dinner
 egg on toast

 fish & chips
 fish and chips
 jacket potato
 lasagne
 lunch

 macaroni cheese
 main course
 meal
 packed lunch
 pastie

 pastry
 picnic
 picnic
 pizza
 quiche

 ravioli
 roast dinner
 sausage and mash
 spaghetti
 starter

 stew
 stir fry
 supper

20.6 Desserts & snacks

Anzac Biscuits	apple yoghurt	apricot yoghurt	banana yoghurt	biscuit
biscuit	blackcurrant yoghurt		cake	candy floss
cherry yoghurt	chocolate	chocolate box	chocolate cake	chocolate egg
chocolate roll	crisps	cupcake	dessert	dessert
doughnut	doughnut	gateau	gingerbread man	ice cream
ice cream	ice lolly	icecream cone	icing	jam roll
jelly	lamington	lemon yoghurt	lolly	meringue
mince pie	mints	orange yoghurt	pancake	pavlova
peach yoghurt	pear yoghurt	pineapple yoghurt	plum yoghurt	popcorn
pudding	pudding	pudding	raspberry yoghurt	sandwich
snack	sponge cake	strawberry yoghurt		sweet
sweets	swiss roll	tea cake	treats	yoghurt

20.7 Sauces herbs & flavours

 bay leaf

 brown sauce

 condiments

 custard

 flavouring

 food colouring

 garnish

 ginger

 gravy

 gravy

 herbs

 ketchup

 mint

 mustard

 parsley

 pepper

 pickles

 puree

 salad cream

 salt

 salt & pepper

 spicy

 vanilla

 vinegar

21 COOKING & EATING

21.1 Objects

 apple corer

baking tray

barbecue

billycan

blender

bottle

bowl

cases

casserole

cauldron

chopping board

chopsticks

cleaver

colander

cooker

cooling tray

cover

cup

cups

cutlery

cutter

dicem

dish

dredger

egg-cup

egg timer

feeder cup

feeding tube

flask

foil

fork

fork

fruit bowl

frying pan

glass

grater

grillpan

hob

ice tray

jug

kitchen equipment

knife

knife

knife

lemon squeezer

lid

masher

measuring jug

microwave

mixer

mug

opener

oven

oven gloves

pan

 peeler	placemat	plate	pressure cooker	recipe
rolling pin	saucer	scourer	sieve	spatula
spoon	spoon	stove	straw	straw
tablespoon	tea towel	teapot	teaspoon	toaster
tray	whisk	wine glass	wok	

21.2 Processes

add	bake	barbecue	beat	blend
boil	boil	break	burn	carve
chip	chop	cook	cook	crumble
decorate	don't microwave	drain	fry	grate
grease	grill	ice	mash	mince
mix	mixture	open	peel	poach
pour	roast	roll	rub	scrape

set

 sieve

 simmer

 slice

 spread

 sprinkle

 steam

 toast marshmallows

21.3 Eating & drinking

 bad taste

 bite

 chew

 delicious

 diet

 drink

 eat

 fast

 feed

 flavour

 good taste

 healthy eating

 hungry

 lick

 suck

 taste

 taste

 thirsty

 thirsty

 vegan

 vegan

 vegetarian

21.4 Catering & restaurants

 bar

 buffet

 cafe

 canteen

 lay table

 lunch box

 menu

 napkin

 napkin ring

 restaurant

 serve

 serving

 table cloth

 take away

22 BUILDINGS

22.1 General

arena	art gallery	building	bungalow	cabin
castle	cathedral	church	church	concert hall
cottage	crematorium	factory	factory	factory
fire station	flat	flats	home	homeless
homes	hostel	hotel	house	house
house	hut	igloo	leisure centre	leisure centre
library	maintenance building	museum	palace	palace
power station	pub	residence	science museum	stores
technology centre	tower	tower block	town hall	

22.2 Specific buildings

Cardiff castle	Downing street	Hogwarts	natural history museum	parliament

parliament house	vatican

22.3 Parts of buildings

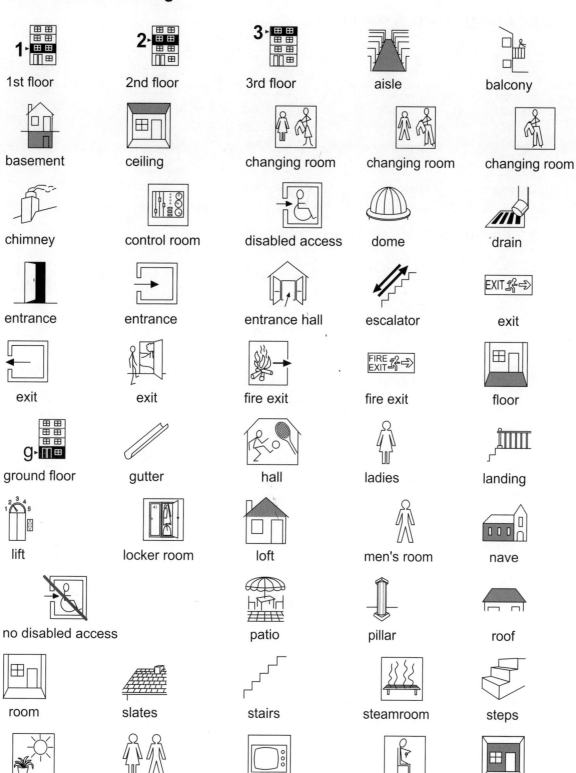

1st floor

2nd floor

3rd floor

aisle

balcony

basement

ceiling

changing room

changing room

changing room

chimney

control room

disabled access

dome

drain

entrance

entrance

entrance hall

escalator

exit

exit

exit

fire exit

fire exit

floor

ground floor

gutter

hall

ladies

landing

lift

locker room

loft

men's room

nave

no disabled access

patio

pillar

roof

room

slates

stairs

steamroom

steps

sunroom

toilets

tv room

waiting room

wall

wall

window

23 HOME, INTERIORS and DOMESTIC ACTIVITIES

23.1 Living places & rooms

bathroom

bedroom

dining room

double room

kitchen

living room

nursery

single room

utility room

23.2 Furniture, fixtures & furnishings

alarm

armchair

bean bag

bed

bedboard

bunk beds

carpet

chair

chair

coat hook

cupboard

curtain

cushion

deckchair

door

door handle

double bed

drawer

dressing table

fireplace

furniture

fuse box

letterbox

light

light bulb

locker

mattress

mosquito net

mural

radiator

rug

seat

settee

shelf

shelves

sideboard

single bed

stool

store

switch

table

tap

wardrobe

waterbed

23.3 Bathroom

bath	bath	bath plug	flush	jacuzzi
plug hole	shower	shower curtain	sink	tiles
toilet	toilet roll	washbasin		

23.4 Kitchen

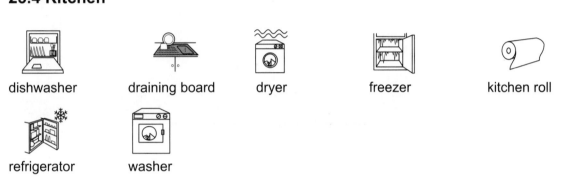

dishwasher	draining board	dryer	freezer	kitchen roll
refrigerator	washer			

23.5 Domestic process

clean room	drain	dust	empty rubbish	hoover
iron	make bed	mop	polish	sweep
wash	washup			

23.6 Domestic items

ashtray	bin	bin bag	blanket	broom

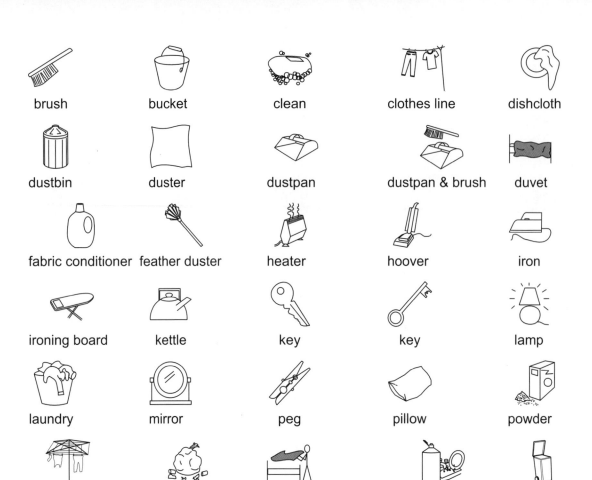

brush	bucket	clean	clothes line	dishcloth
dustbin	duster	dustpan	dustpan & brush	duvet
fabric conditioner	feather duster	heater	hoover	iron
ironing board	kettle	key	key	lamp
laundry	mirror	peg	pillow	powder
rotary dryer	rubbish bag	sheet	washing-up liquid	wheelie bin

23.7 Babycare & baby equipment

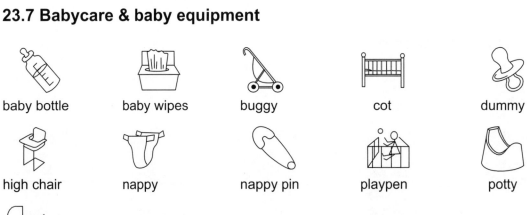

baby bottle	baby wipes	buggy	cot	dummy
high chair	nappy	nappy pin	playpen	potty
pram				

24 WORK and EQUIPMENT

24.1 Work & jobs vocabulary

career

employ

job centre

job search

office work

wages

wages

work

work experience

workroom

workshop

24.2 General tools, work items & actions

9-volt battery

battery

anvil

axe

battery

beam

brick

buzzer

cable

cable

cement mixer

chisel

crane

drill

extension lead

file

filter

fork-lift

funnel

hammer

hammer

hook

insulation

ladder

lamp

lathe

light holder

machine

mallet

nail

net

padlock

paint

paintbrush

part

plaster

pliers

plug

plug

plug

 plumbing

 propeller

 sandpaper

 saw

 screw

 screwdriver

 shovel

 socket

 socket (Aus)

 solar panel

 spanner

 spring

 step ladder

 t-square

 tools

 trowel

 wallpaper

 wire

25 PACKAGING

25. 1 Container types

bag	basket	bottle	box	carton
containers	crate	jar	packet	plastic bottle
sack	spray can	tin		

25. 2 Containers

lid	milk carton

25. 3 Containers specific

cool box	stubbie	stubbie holder

25. 4 Actions

wrap

26 SHOPS, SHOPPING and ORGANISATIONS

26.1 Small shops

 antique shop

 baby shop

 bag shop

 bakers

 barbers

 beauty salon

betting shop

bike shop

 book shop

bread shop

butchers

camping shop

card shop

carpet shop

casino

 cd shop

 charity shop

 chemist

 clothes shop

 corner shop

 dairy

 delicatessen

 dress shop

 electrical shop

 electrical shop

 estate agent

 fish and chips

 flower shop

 furniture shop

 general shop

 gift shop

 greengrocers

 grocers

 haberdashery shop

 hairdressers

 healthfood shop

 jewellers

 kitchen shop

 newsagent

 off licence

 pet shop

 pizza house

 post office

 record shop

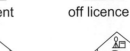 sandwich shop

 shoe shop

shop

shops

 sports shop

 stationers

 sweet shop

 sweet shop

 ticket office

 toy shop

 travel agent

travel agents

tv shop

26.2 Large shops

car showroom

department store

DIY store

garden centre

shopping centre

supermarket

26.3 Shopping & prices

bargain

bill

bring and buy

buy

buy

car boot sale

cash register

cheap

cheaper

cheapest

checkout

closed

cost

expensive

free

how much

open

receipt

sell

shopping

special offer

trolley

vending machine

25.4 Specific shops & logos

Adams

Argos

Asda

Etam

gateway

Gateway

Guides

M&S

Marks & Spencer

McDonald's

mencap

Mencap

National Lottery

Red Cross

 Safeway

 Scouts

TESCO Tesco

widgit widget

25.5 Organisations

 accountants

 airline

 arts council

 business

 car company

 charity

 computer company

 electricity company

 environment agency

 gas company

 gateway club

 graphic design company

 health authority

 internet company

 mobile phone company

 NASA

 NHS

 organisation

 PHAB

 pharmaceutical company

 phone company

 publisher

 recruitment company

 RSPB

 RSPCA

 television company

 water company

27 MONEY

27. 1 Currency

$1

$10

$2

$20

$5

$50

10c

20c

50 cents

1 pound

10 pounds

100 pounds

10p

1p

2 pounds

20 pounds

20p

2p

5 pence

5 pounds

50 pence

50 pounds

£10

£100

euro

27.2 Money

Australian money

coin

coins

currency

money

note

27.3 Banking, handling money & taxes

accounts

allowance

bank

bank card

building society

car tax

cash point

change

cheque

council tax

credit card

cuts

borrow

exchange

expenses

fare

fine

fund raise

hire

income tax

lottery

my money

national insurance

no money

offering

pay

poor

rich

save money

school fees

spend

tax

treasurer

VAT

28 TRANSPORT

28.1 Vehicles

 aeroplane

 ambulance

 articulated lorry

 barge

 bicycle

 boat

 boat

 bulldozer

 bus

 canoe

 car

 caravan

 caravan

 cars

 catamaran

 coach

 digger

 double decker

 dumper truck

 dustcart

 electric train

 excavator

 ferry

 fire engine

 four wheeled drive

 giant dumper

 hearse

 helicopter

 hovercraft

 juggernaut

 light aircraft

 lorry

 milk float

 minibus

 motor bike

 motor boat

 mountain bike

 pedalo

 people carrier

 pickup truck

 police car

 road sweeper

 rocket

 school bus

 scooter

 ship

 space shuttle

 steam train

 taxi

 tipper lorry

 tractor

 train

 train

 train

 transport

trawler

 tricycle

 tube train

 van

 vehicle

28.2 Vehicle parts

 bell

 bike chain

 bike pump

 bonnet

 boot

 brake

 buffer

 bus doors

 bus lift

 bus schedule

 car door

 car engine

 car tyre

 car window

 coupling

 engine

 handle bars

 jack

 mast

 motor

 pedals

 saddle

 seat

 seats

 transport equipment

 tyre

 wheel

28.3 Road signs

 cross roads

 crossing

 give way

 junction

kangaroo crossing

 koala crossing

 level crossing

 no entry

 road sign

 roundabout

 signpost

 traffic lights

114

28.4 Places & events

 air show

 airport

 bus station

 bus stop

 car park

 car wash

 carport

 cruise

 garage

 garage

 hangar

 motor show

 multi-story

platform

station

station

28.5 Travel vocabulary

 accident

 brake

 car fumes

 crash

 diesel

 drive

 driver

 driving licence

 go by bus

 go by car

 go by plane

 go by train

 journey

 land

 land

  minibus maintenance

 outing

 park

 passport

 passport

 petrol

 petrol pump

 rails

 railway

 road safety

 route

 safety belt

 take off

 take off

 traffic

 traffic control

 train timetable

 travel

 wash car

29 KNOWLEDGE and COMMUNICATION

29.1 Thinking & learning

abilities

able

agree

agree

believe

can't decide

change

choice

choose

class

clever

difficult

disagree

disagree

don't know

don't know

dream

easy

fantasy

feel

forget

forgive

group work

guess

idea

indecision

know

learn

maybe

mental skill

misunderstand

nightmare

office skills

predict

pretend

pretend

probably

probably not

problem

read

reader

relationship skills

remember

remind

research

research

skill

spell

success

teach

think

training

training

which one

wish

write

writer

29.2 Gestures

clap

encourage

hold hands

hug

kiss

kiss

nod

point

shake

sign

sign language

wave

yawn

29.3 Expressions

best wishes

good job

goodbye

greet

hello

leave me alone

no

ok

ok

ok

please

shove off

shut up

sorry

thank

welcome

yes

you're crazy

29.4 Values

bad

bad

best

better

blame

correct

don't love

duty

good

good luck

honour

how

important

improve

lie

lucky

must

nosy

not

promise

respect

special

true

trust

truth

worse

worst

wrong

29.5 Communication

abuse

address

allow

allow

answer

apologise

argue

ask

attention

call

chat

communicate

communicate

communication

communication helper

describe

don't scream

don't tell

dumb

explain

hear

introduce

invite

joke

name

non-speaking

not allowed

ouch

repeat

say

say

say

scream

secret

show me

speak

speak word

speech

speech and language	swear	symbol	talk
tell	tell	vocalise	whisper	who
whose	whose	yell		

29.6 Communication aids & access

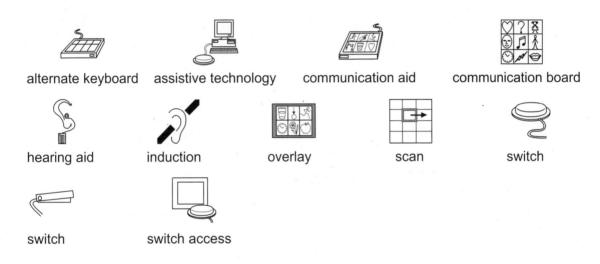

alternate keyboard	assistive technology	communication aid	communication board
hearing aid	induction	overlay	scan	switch
switch	switch access			

29.7 Media & phone

answer	call	CCTV	helpline	media
mobile phone	mobile phone battery	mobile phone buttons	mobile phone case
mobile phone charger	mobile phone covers	mobile phone screen	no pagers
no phones	pager	radio	ring tones	telephone
telephone box	text message	wap		

29.8 Computer & internet

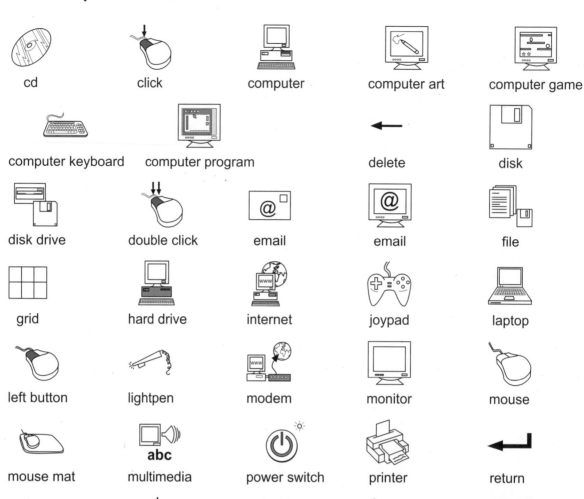

cd	click	computer	computer art	computer game
computer keyboard	computer program		delete	disk
disk drive	double click	email	email	file
grid	hard drive	internet	joypad	laptop
left button	lightpen	modem	monitor	mouse
mouse mat	multimedia	power switch	printer	return
right button	right click	touch screen	type	windows

Writing with Symbols

29.9 Computer icons

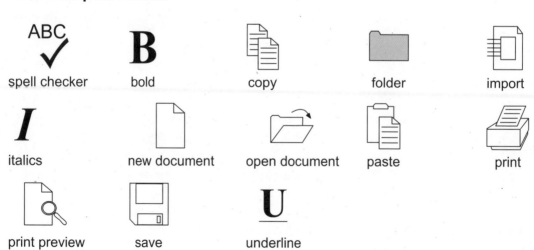

spell checker	bold	copy	folder	import
italics	new document	open document	paste	print
print preview	save	underline		

120

29.10 Icons for use in Writing with Symbols 2000

delete

enter

F12

more

print

speak

speech

repeat speech

exit

29.11 Mail

address

Dear

deliver

letter

parcel

post

post code

postbag

postcard

reply

sorting office

stamp

stamp

zip code

29.12 News & information

health information

information

information

information centre

leaflet

magazine

map

news

news

newspaper

poster

safety information

telephone information

travel information

TV times

30 EDUCATION and OFFICE

30.1 Places

 adult education

 assembly

 assembly hall

 classroom

 college

 hall

 IT centre

 IT room

 junior school

 light room

 meeting room

 music room

 nursery school

 office

 office

 open university

 reception

 residential college

 school

 secondary school

 staff room

 study

 technology room

 technology room

30.2 Subjects

 art

 art class

 art class

 biology

 chemistry

 course

 education

 English

 English lesson

 food technology

 geography

 history

 home economics class

 IT

 language

 lesson

 literacy

 maths

 maths lesson

 metalwork

 music and movement

 music class

 pe

 physics

 science

 science lesson

 sex education

 subjects

 technology

technology

technology lesson

woodwork

30.3 Office & educational equipment

abacus

box file

certificate

chalk

copier

crayon

desk

display board

drawing pins

eraser

fax

felt tips

folder

globe

lectern

notice board

paper

paper clip

paste

paste brush

pe post

pen

pencil

pencil

pencil lead

pencil sharpener

picture book

plastic wallet

rack

ring binder

rubber band

school bag

sellotape

stamp

stamp

stapler

stationary

sticking

superglue

typewriter

30.4 Writing & documents

application

autobiography

biography

book

catalogue

colour

comic

cross out

cut & paste

design

diary	diary	dictionary	document	draw
fiction	letter	library card	lined paper	message
notebook	notepad	notes	page	pamphlet
pencil case	poem	readable	report card	rub out
scribble	sentence	shopping list	sketchbook	work plan

30.5 Grammar

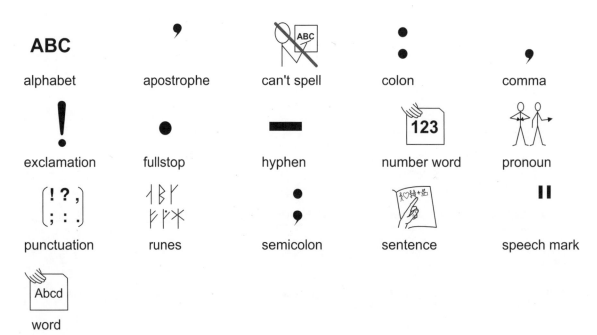

ABC	apostrophe	can't spell	colon	comma
alphabet				
exclamation	fullstop	hyphen	number word	pronoun
punctuation	runes	semicolon	sentence	speech mark
word				

30.6 Letters

All letters of the alphabet are available in upper and lower cases.

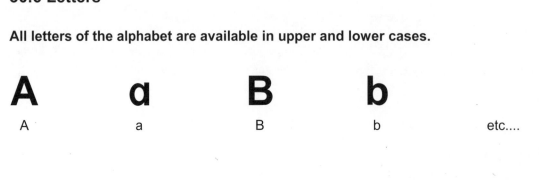

A	a	B	b	etc....

30.7 Events & times

absent

conference

enrol

field trip

homework

in school

interview

lecture

no school

school holiday

speech

study

term

quiz

31 COMMUNITY and SOCIAL

31.1 Places

community centre

community home

community homes

creche

day centre

disabled home

public

31.2 Advocacy, record keeping & planning

achieve

action plan

advice

adviser

advocacy

advocacy group

advocate

against the rules

agenda

agreement

audit

campaign

chairperson

charter

committee

committee member

complain

complaints procedure

conference

consult

consultation

delegate

disabled rights

draft plan

empower

equality

equality

exclude

fair

feedback

form

health advice

id card

inclusion

independent

individual plan

integration

integrate

joint strategy

list

mark

matters arising

meeting

minutes · national record · not fair · personal plan · privacy

private · protect · protected money · record · reference

represent · review · rights · rules · self advocacy

speak up · special plan · strategy

31.3 Social services

group house · member · service user · services · social services

31.4 Care

assess · care for · care plan · care plan · carer

case conference · family adviser · helping hand · home help · key worker

personal adviser · personal helper · respite · safe place · unit

volunteer

31. 5 Government, politics & law

 arrest

 election

 elections

 emergency

 emergency services

 European minister

 european ministers

 government

 government building

 Green party

 handcuffs

 illegal

 labour

 law

 LibDem

 local authority

 party

 police

 police station

 police station

 prime minister

 prison

 prisoner

 probation

 probation officer

 scale of justice

 vote

 will

31.7 War & fighting

 armed services

 armies

 bomb

 dagger

 gun

 soldier

 soldiers

 sword

 terrorist

 torpedo

31.8 Processes, events & related items

 coffin

 cremate

 cremation

 exhibition

 funeral

 grave

 headstone

 mourn

 opportunities

31.9 Awards

 1st place

 award

 award

 award scheme

 bronze medal

 congratulate

 medal

 prize

 silver medal

 trophy

32 CELEBRATIONS and GREETING CARDS

32.1 Events & activities

birthday

birthday

celebrate

celebrate

Christmas

corroboree

Easter

happy birthday

parade

party

silver wedding

trick or treat

wedding

32.2 Objects

baby card

banner

birthday cake

birthday card

card

card

Christmas cake

Christmas card

christmas stocking

Christmas tree

cracker

decorations

get well card

good luck card

party hat

present

stocking

tinsel

valentine

wedding cake

wreath

33 SCIENCE MATHS

33.1 General terms

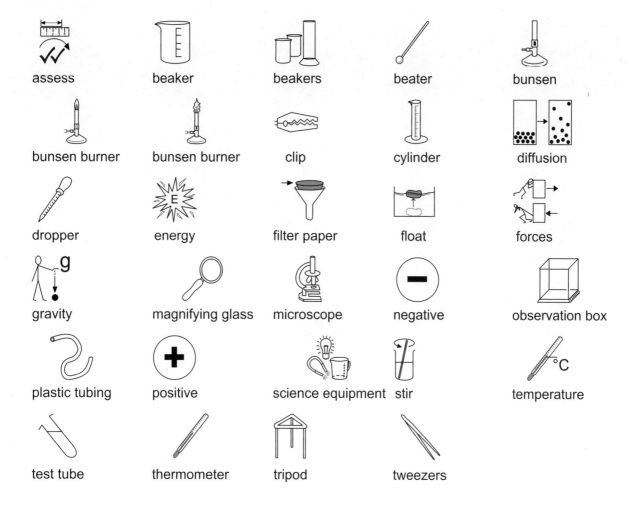

assess   beaker   beakers   beater   bunsen

bunsen burner   bunsen burner   clip   cylinder   diffusion

dropper   energy   filter paper   float   forces

gravity   magnifying glass   microscope   negative   observation box

plastic tubing   positive   science equipment   stir   temperature

test tube   thermometer   tripod   tweezers

33.2 Physics

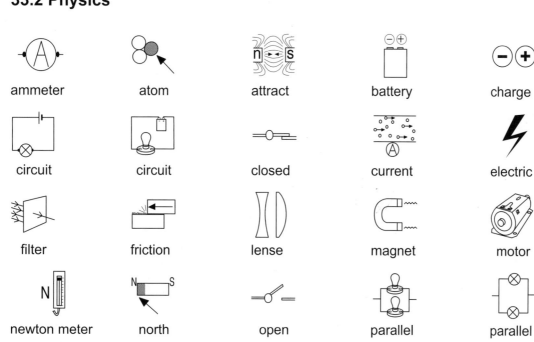

ammeter   atom   attract   battery   charge

circuit   circuit   closed   current   electric

filter   friction   lense   magnet   motor

newton meter   north   open   parallel   parallel

prism

 pull meter

 radiate

 refract

 series

 series

 south pole

 spectrum

 switch

 voltage

 voltmeter

33.3 Chemistry

 pH1→6
acid

 pH8→14
alkali

 alkaline

 bond

 double bond

 halogens

 ionic bond

 ions

 lattice

 molecule

pH7
neutral

nobel gas

33.4 Biology

 absorb

 amniotic fluid

 amniotic sac

 anther

 anvil

 artery

 atrium

 axon

 butterfly life cycle

 cell body

 chambers

 chicken life cycle

 chromosome

 cilla

 CO2

 cochlea

 cornea

 dendtites

 diaphragm

 DNA

 ear drum

 eggs

 embryo

 eye

 fallopian tube

filament

flower

foetus

frog life cycle

gamete

genes

hair follicle

hammer

heart

hip bone

hooks

inner ear

intestines

iris

joint

kidneys

large intestine

lens

life cycle

lungs

muscle

muscles

myelin sheath

neucleus

neuron

node of ranvier

offspring

optic nerve

organs

ovary

oxygen producers

parents

pelvis

petri dish

photosynthesis

pistil

placenta

pollenate

protein

pump

receptors

red blood cells

reproduce

retina

sacs

secrete

semicircular canals

small intestine

stamen

stigma

stirrup

style

sweat gland

sweat pore

trachea

transpire

tubes

umbilical cord

veins

veins

ventricle

33.5 Maths

3+1+2=

add

$$\begin{array}{r} 2 \\ +3 \\ \hline 5 \end{array}$$

answer

audit

calculator

count

countdown

diagram

4÷2=

divide

graph

graph

graph

graph

3×2=

multiply

3−1−2=

subtract

34 HISTORY

34.1 People

 caveman

 knight

 maid

 soldier

 viking

 warrior

34.2 Artefacts

 arrow

 bow and arrow

 butter pats

 cave painting

 coach

 corset

 crinoline

 Endeavour

 flat iron

 gaslight

 grindstone

 helmet

 lantern

 long ship

 mangle

 oil lamp

 oil lamp

 oil lamp

 pocket watch

 quern

 range

 scrubbing board

 shield

 shield

 slate

 sling

 spear

 spinning wheel

 tin bath

 totem pole

 urn

 washstand

 washtub

 water pouch

 water pump

 weapon

34.3 Historical periods & events

egyptian

middle ages

pre-historic

roman

vikings

34.4 Actions & activities

joust

35 RELIGION

35.1 General or multi-faith

angel

ark

blessing

church window

God

God

Goliath

guru

hassock

heaven

holy

holy spirit

hymn

icon

peace

pew

praise

pray

pulpit

religion

trinity

vestment

35.2 Christian

advent calendar

altar

apostle

baby Jesus

baptise

baptism

Baptist

Bethlehem

bible

bishop

chapel

Christ

Christ

christening dress

Christian

communion

Easter

Epiphany

Eucharist

font

godfather

godmother

gospel

Holy Spirit

holy week

jesus

joseph

lent

magi

manger

mary

 maundy thursday

 minister

 minister

 minister

 monk

 nativity

 new testament

 nun

 palm sunday

 pope

 pray

 prayer book

 preach

 resurrection

 rosary

 saint

 shrine

 sunday school

35.3 Jewish

 ark

 bar mitzvah

 bat mitzvah

 challah

 gregger

 Haggadah

 Hanukkah

 holy book

 kippah

 magen david

 menorah

 mezuzah

 mezuzah

 pray

 rabbi

 synagogue

 tallit

 torah

35.4 Hindu

 Bhagavad Gita

 bhajan

 Hindu

 Hindu food

 holy book

 krishna

 mandir

 pray

 priest

ramayana

rig veda

shrine

35.5 Muslim

Allah

Allah

 holy book

 imam

 islam

 koran

 makkah

 minbar

 mosque

 pray

wu du

35.6 Sikh

 five ks

 Granthi

 gudwala

 gurdwara

 holy book

 kachera

 kangha

 kara

kesh

kirpan

 mala

 pray

 shrine

sikh

35.7 Buddhist

 Buddha

 Buddhist

 holy book

 pray

 priest

 shrine

 sutta

 temple

36 MISCELLANEOUS

36.1 Miscellaneous abstract vocabulary

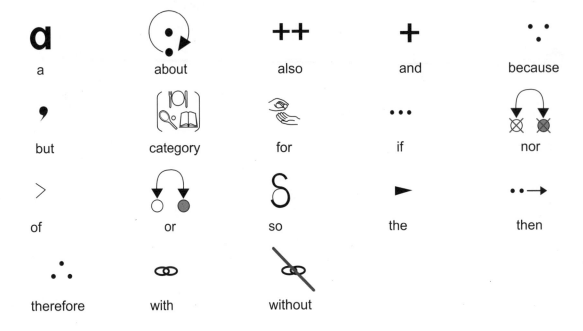

a	about	also	and	because
but	category	for	if	nor
of	or	so	the	then
therefore	with	without		

36.2 Miscellaneous pronouns

this	that	these	those	the one

36.3 Questions

questions	questions	what's wrong

Some words are used simply to indicate a question. In this case an abstract image of the questionmark would normally be the most appropriate symbol.

do	how	why

36.4 Miscelaneous adjectives

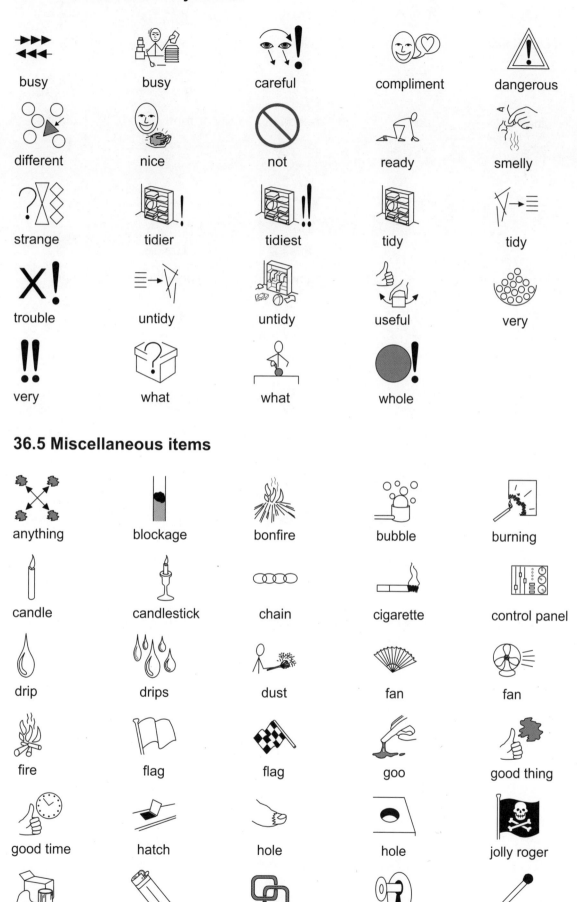

busy	busy	careful	compliment	dangerous
different	nice	not	ready	smelly
strange	tidier	tidiest	tidy	tidy
trouble	untidy	untidy	useful	very
very	what	what	whole	

36.5 Miscellaneous items

anything	blockage	bonfire	bubble	burning
candle	candlestick	chain	cigarette	control panel
drip	drips	dust	fan	fan
fire	flag	flag	goo	good thing
good time	hatch	hole	hole	jolly roger
junk	lighter	link	lock	match

megaphone

 mess

 mirror

 mistake

 ornament

 pipe

 rack

 ribbon

 rope

 rubbish

 rubbish

 safety pin

 scissors

 shock

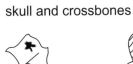 skull and crossbones

 some thing

 some things

 spot

 stain

 string

 surprise

 the one

 thing

 things

 things

 things

 ticket

torch

 tray

 vase

 which one

142